INVENTIVE GENIUS

INVENTIVE GENIUS

By the Editors of Time-Life Books

TIME-LIFE BOOKS, ALEXANDRIA, VIRGINIA

CONTENTS

THE INVENTORS

The purpose of invention, a great scientific pioneer once said, is "the complete mastery of mind over the material world." The words may evoke a race of innovative, power-seeking titans, but most inventors merely serve necessity, the proverbial mother of invention. These women and men have a knack for finding problems and then solving them in a unique way.

The very names of some inventors, such as Leonardo da Vinci and Thomas Alva Edison, have become synonyms for inventive creativity. Others have achieved enduring fame in the common names of such things as diesels, Levi's, and leotards. And many, cursed by bad timing or the greed of powerful competitors, have toiled without recognition in their lifetimes. But their differences are less important than their shared characteristics. Acknowledged innovator or struggling unknown, these creators of new methods and machines tend toward uncommon practicality and persistence, fired by the unpredictable, eccentric spark that is inventive genius.

Renaissance Man

Painter. Sculptor. Architect. Military engineer. Natural scientist. Inventor. No one has matched the sweep of talents displayed by Leonardo da Vinci, possibly the most inventive man of all time. But his brilliance had a stunning flaw: He rarely finished what he started; often he did not start at all.

Leonardo's reputation rests less on his achievements than on his prescient good intentions. His surviving notebooks—thousands of pages of beautifully executed diagrams and notes, written right to left and backwards—preserve his ideas on everything from drainage projects to war machines and human flight. In these pages, Leonardo created a double-hulled ship, a forerunner of the modern military tank, a radical new system of fortification, metal-rolling machines, thrust bearings, mechanical cooking spits, chain links, an improved breechloading cannon, and other precocious concepts.

Most of his designs were never built, and some were copied from elsewhere. His helicopter, for example, may have been based on a children's toy. Even in his own era, he was described as "capricious and fickle." But the same restless intelligence that annoyed detractors made him, in the words of a biographer, "the most relentlessly curious man in history."

Little is known of Leonardo's personal life. He was born in Vinci in 1452, the illegitimate son of a landowner who became a notary to the aristocracy of nearby Florence. His father gave him a good education, although young Leonardo did not do well in Latin. He was, by all accounts, very handsome, and strong: He could bend a horseshoe with his hands. When Leonardo was about fourteen, his father apprenticed him to Andrea del Verrocchio, one of Italy's foremost painters and sculptors.

Leonardo spent six years with Verrocchio and soon began to outshine his master as a painter. At the same time, he displayed a fascination with mechanics and engineering, offering schemes for draining marshes, taming the Arno River with canals, and designing flour mills. Two potent talents already lay behind his ideas: the ability to identify the simple essences of complicated things and the skill to combine those fundamental elements in new and unexpected ways—especially when using machines to multiply the power of human labor.

His inventive genius rested on real as well as figurative vision, however. Leonardo had a remarkable eye for detailed motion. Only centuries afterward did it become clear just how sharp his eye really was. For example, he was able to discern the chaotic patterns within swirling water, turbulent motions not revealed to ordinary humans until the advent of the slow-motion camera. This rare acuity allowed him to study

the dynamics of winged flight in unprecedented detail.

Around 1477, Leonardo left Verrocchio's studio and set up one of his own. Once installed and working, however, he received a cold shock: He was passed over when artists were selected to work in the Vatican. Stung by the insult to his talent, he moved to Milan in 1482, hoping for the patronage of the ruling duke, Ludovico Sforza.

Cruel, suspicious, and miserly, Ludovico was interested in art less for its aesthetic value than for the prestige it conferred. But, faced with the constant warfare waged by the Italian city-states, he needed military engineers more than artists. Leonardo thus sold himself with notebooks bursting with bellicose ideas: a new, rounded form of fortress architecture that was more resistant to cannonballs; a rapid-firing gun; the first wheel-lock firearm; the first streamlined missiles with tail fins.

Leonardo's tenure in Milan produced his Last Supper fresco, along with the hygrometer, which he invented to monitor the humidity around his moisture-sensitive painting. But his stay lasted only as long as the Sforzas, who were driven out by the French in 1499. Without a patron, Leonardo moved on to Mantua, then Venice, where he invented a diving apparatus with a snorkel attachment for use against the Turkish fleet. The next four years, he wandered in and out of Florence, serving, among others, the rapacious Cesare Borgia. This was the period of his coexistence with Michelangelo, who despised him, and of his creation of the world's best-known painting, the *Mona Lisa*. Typically, Leonardo stopped work on a larger commission to do the portrait. When Florence's council complained, he returned to Milan.

But the new century held little promise for Leonardo. The fortunes of war again left him in Milan without a patron, and his physical powers were on the wane. He traveled to the Vatican and won a small painting commission but lost it when he spent his time trying to create a new kind of varnish for the work. Some historians believe he may have suffered a stroke during this period. His only self-portrait shows a man sadly and prematurely aged beyond his sixty years. He was rescued from complete poverty by King Francis I of France, who invited Leonardo to the court at Amboise.

There he died in 1519, having completed his last drawings: apocalyptic visions of the world destroyed by a great deluge. He left his notebooks to an apprentice, but they were eventually dispersed. And even in death, Leonardo could not dodge war's fortunes. In later conflicts, the Amboise graves were uprooted, the bodies interred in a common grave. Remains said to be Leonardo's were put on display in a chapel beside the castle at Amboise, but they cannot be authenticated. His notebooks, and his remarkably clear perception of a world to come, are all that remain of the great imaginer. □

Peering from his only self-portrait, an aged Leonardo da Vinci seems to contemplate two inventive visions of his youth: a deadly military chariot *(far left)* with revolving blades to rend and dismember soldiers in its path; and a fanciful flying saucer *(near left)*, powered by a double set of paddlelike wings turned by a standing pilot.

Using the power of steam and a series of pulleys and siphons, Hero invented a device that spun an illusion of magic: As a priest lit the fire, the temple doors would open automatically.

Greek Hero

Much of what is known today of ancient technology comes from the writings of a single man, Hero—or Heron—of Alexandria. "When his name and the place of his abode have been given," wrote one nineteenth-century translator, "all that can be positively affirmed is exhausted." It is not even known whether Hero was the preeminent inventor of his age or a chronicler of the inventions of others.

He lived in the first century AD, one of a distinguished group who came to the famed Alexandria Museum, then a center of Greco-Roman scholarship. Much of what remains of his writings is found in a body of work called *Pneumatica*. He also produced treatises on the construction of catapults and crossbows, methods of lifting heavy bodies, and a "spying tube" called a *dioptra*, an early version of the surveyor's transit.

Although it is not always clear which creations were actually his, Hero is considered the inventor of, among other things, a steam turbine, a syringe, an odometer, a wind vane, and a coin-operated dispenser for holy water.

Hero echoed the profound fascination of Greek culture with the mechanical world. But philosophy, not necessity, was the mother of Greek invention: There was little interest in the practical products that could be derived from some of the ingenious devices. In fact, much of what Hero described took the form not of great machines but of toys and effects, among them temple doors rigged to open automatically when a priest ignited a sacred fire; mechanisms on which dancers twirled and birds whistled; and a steam-driven jet that whirled like a pinwheel.

Oddly, Hero's innovations went largely ignored even by the engineering-minded Romans. Steam-driven devices that could have multiplied the power of human labor many times remained no more than playthings. The reason was not technological. In a society based on abundant slave labor, there was no incentive to develop laborsaving machines. □

An Electrifying Intellect

One stormy day in June 1752, a plump, bespectacled man in his midforties launched a kite into the turbulent sky over Philadelphia. The solitary figure of Benjamin Franklin linked to lightning by a thin line, a silk kite, and a metal key has since become one of the enduring symbols of individual research. Aimed at proving Franklin's belief that lightning is merely a massive form of electricity, the experiment succeeded brilliantly. Bright sparks leaped from the electrified key to Franklin's fingertips, verifying that the thunderbolt was electrical in nature.

Contrary to popular belief, this dangerous kite flight came near the end, not at the beginning, of Franklin's invention of the science of electricity. Five years earlier, the affluent printer, inventor, and writer of pithy sayings had acquired the means to retire. At about the same time, an electrical demonstration performed at his Market Street home had ignited a fierce interest in Franklin, which was kindled further by an English friend's gift of a yard-long glass tube that gave off static sparks. "I never was before engaged in any study that so totally engrossed my attention and my time," Franklin wrote later.

In some ways, he was an unlikely candidate for scientific invention. Born in Boston, the fifteenth of seventeen Franklin children from his father's two marriages, Franklin received scant formal education. He polished his keen intellect through voracious reading. By age twelve, he was publishing verse and, not long afterward, essays.

In this detail of a heroic rendering, Benjamin Franklin reaches out to a lightning-charged key held aloft by a storm-tossed kite—an enduring image of the man who, using such instruments as the Electro-static machine shown below, invented the science of electricity.

Apprenticed in 1718 to his brother James, a Boston printer, he ran away at seventeen, first to New York, then to Philadelphia. He returned briefly to Boston a year later, then moved to London to work as a printer, the trade he pursued upon his return to Philadelphia in 1726. In about 1740, he designed the famous Franklin stove, which, like other Franklin inventions (such as bifocal glasses), he declined to patent.

When he began his electrical studies in 1748, Franklin, always an indifferent mathematician, lacked such tools as calculus to analyze his findings. Instead, he followed a tortuous trial-and-error procedure to his pioneering conclusion: Electricity is a single force with positive and negative aspects. His discovery was described 200 years later as the "most fundamental thing done" in the field. Feeling, as he put it to a friend, "a Want of Terms," Franklin also invented the vocabulary of electricity: *charged, armature, conductor,* and *battery* were among some twenty-five terms he created to describe his work. He was knocked unconscious twice during his experiments: once when treating a paralyzed patient with electric shock and again while trying to kill a turkey with electricity.

Convinced by 1749 of "the sameness of lightning with electricity," he designed a hair-raisingly dangerous experiment to prove it. "On the Top of some high Tower or Steeple," he wrote, "place a Kind of Sentry Box big enough to contain a Man and an electrical Stand. From the Middle of the Stand let an Iron Rod rise . . . upright 20 or 30 feet, pointed very sharp at the End." A man standing in the box "when such Clouds are passing low, might be electrified and afford sparks, the Rod drawing Fire to him from the Cloud."

The experiment was performed in France in May 1752, without harming the researchers. But a Swedish scholar working in Russia was less fortunate: Lightning killed George Wilhelm Richman when he tried to follow Franklin's scheme. Ignorant of the French experimentation, in 1752 Franklin and his son, William, launched a silk kite into a Pennsylvania storm. But fame as the world's preeminent "electrician" was already in hand. The year before, his compiled letters to an English colleague had been published as *Experiments and Observations in Electricity.* Translated abroad in 1752, the volume made Franklin a famous man—and paved the way for his final career as diplomat. He had long been a hero of invention to the French when he went to Paris as one of three American commissioners to France in 1776.

After stepping down from public service, Franklin continued to innovate. He developed a mechanical arm for taking books from shelves and invented what he felt was his most important device: a flexible catheter to ease the pain caused by the kidney stones that plagued him until his death in 1790. □

Metal Rain

In 1784, looking for a way to make artillery more devastating to advancing infantry, a young second lieutenant in Britain's Royal Artillery hit on the idea of filling a canister shell with musket balls and a small charge of gunpowder. The canister would explode in flight to spread the smaller rounds for hundreds of yards along the original trajectory, with deadly effect. It took thousands of pounds to perfect the invention, and twenty years for the British to adopt it. But the deadly shell quickly changed warfare and was used against Napoleon at Waterloo. The inventor never received a penny for his invention and was never reimbursed for his considerable out-of-pocket expenses. Promoted to lieutenant general in 1837, he died five years later, aged eighty-one, as Sir Henry Shrapnel. His name lives on, but not as a kind of ammunition. *Shrapnel* has become the term for the jagged metal fragments of any high-explosive shell. □

Steamed!

Few men worked longer or harder to replace human labor with steam power than an American prodigy named Oliver Evans, and few were more poorly rewarded for their efforts. Today a virtual unknown, Evans, more than anyone else, put the steam engine to work in the New World.

Born in 1755, Evans was the fifth of twelve children of Charles Evans, a genteel shoemaker in Newport, Delaware. After what appears to have been a good private education, Evans was apprenticed at sixteen to a wheelwright. He quickly showed a mechanical aptitude, drawing up plans for new kinds of horse-drawn carriages and inventing a way of manufacturing the iron-toothed combs used in carding wool. This invention introduced Evans to the difficulty of finding support for any new creation—and to commercial piracy. Thousands of wool cards were produced from Philadelphia to Boston without a penny to the inventor.

By the 1780s, Evans had taken an interest in flour milling. At the time, American millers—like European ones—were using techniques that involved many hand operations with shovels and rakes, and workers often stomped across the grain with their dirty feet. Evans figured out a cleaner and more efficient process, and in 1785, he and his brothers built America's first automated flour mill.

In the Evans mill, water-powered machinery—with the aid of one man—moved grain through the drying, grinding, spreading, and sorting processes. Evans's invention produced more flour than an old-fashioned miller with two assistants could from the same amount of wheat. Yet when he tried to sell his invention to the tradition-minded millers and plantation owners of the Eastern seaboard, he had only a few takers, George Washington among them. In 1790, Evans acquired a fourteen-year patent on his mill, which began to produce income.

But his real fascination was with the uses of steam, and he sank his mill profits into building a better steam engine. As early as 1772, only three years after Scottish inventor James Watt patented his steam engine, Evans had decided engines such as Watt's—which did not use the great energy of highly compressed steam—would not be powerful enough to do heavy work, and he dreamed of an engine strong enough to propel a wagon.

His first design, completed in 1794, operated at five to eight times the steam pressure of Watt's earlier engine. Evans shipped the designs to England in an unsuccessful bid for a British patent, while a Cornish rival, Richard Trevithick, made a similar breakthrough to power the world's first locomotive and won the patents.

At the turn of the century, Evans finally perfected a small, high-pressure engine and used it to power a grinding wheel rather than a wagon. The device pounded twelve tons of gypsum into plaster of Paris in twenty-four hours and finally drew public attention to his laborsaving machines.

Slowly, Evans's engines began to be used more widely and to grow in size and power. In 1805, the city of Philadelphia offered $3,000 if he could build a power dredge that would clean the city's fouled waterfront. Evans agreed and built a flat-bottomed scow he called *Orukter Amphibolos* (Greek for "Amphibious Digger"). He used steam to power the boat as well as the dredge. When it came time to bring the crude paddle wheeler to the water, he fitted the "Digger" with wheels and drove it to the Schuylkill River, making it the first powered land vehicle in America. (A French steam-powered tricycle designed by Captain Nicolas-Joseph Cugnot in 1769 had been the first in the world.)

Evans's expanding steam engine business kept him busy, but he was frustrated by patent theft and lack of guarantees for an inventor's cre-

ations. In 1805, the U.S. Congress refused to renew his 1791 flour-mill patent, a ruling that left him unprotected until the decision was reversed three years later. During that interval, many millers pirated the system, including Thomas Jefferson's overseer at Monticello. (Jefferson duly paid Evans, whose profit making he abhorred, $89.60 for the infringement.)

But worse was yet to come. In 1809, a Philadelphia court ruled that all patent holders were in violation of public rights. Incensed, and with his horrified family watching, Evans threw the plans for his inventions into the fire. He wrote later, "It was highly dangerous to leave my papers to lead any of my children or grand children into the same road to ruin, that had subjected me to insult, to abuse and robbery all my life." When the ruling was overturned a short time later, Evans patiently reconstructed the drawings he had destroyed. By 1814, Evans's engines were powering cotton and textile mills, grinding minerals,

and powering vessels. But the inventor was wearing out. In 1819, he was seriously ill with pneumonia when word came that his Philadelphia engine factory—what he fondly called his Mars Works—had been destroyed by fire. He died soon afterward.

The *Pittsburgh Gazette* eulogized him as a man who "will be remembered by a nation's gratitude, when the comparatively insignificant herd of metaphysicians and conquerors shall have passed into total oblivion." In fact, it was Oliver Evans who passed into oblivion, a largely forgotten genius of American invention. □

Designed by Oliver Evans *(above, left)* **in 1805,** *Orukter Amphibolos* **(Amphibious Digger) was the first steam-powered land-sea vehicle in the New World. Evans charged viewers twenty-five cents to watch** *Orukter* **in action.**

Fitch Out of Water

Few inventors have been more revered than Robert Fulton, immortalized for his invention of the steamboat. In fact, another man—an obscure failure named John Fitch—developed a workable passenger steamship a full twenty years before Fulton's famous *Clermont* chugged up the Hudson River in 1807.

Born on a Windsor, Connecticut, farm in 1743, Fitch led a varied life. He apprenticed to a clockmaker, skipped in and out of the American revolutionary militia, and went land surveying in Kentucky and Ohio, where he was captured by Indians in 1782 and traded to the British. While a prisoner of war, Fitch attained a kind of creative pinnacle, earning a living and some reputation from woodcarving and engraving portraits of British officers. Eventually exchanged, he worked for a time as a surveyor.

In Pennsylvania in 1785, Fitch was inspired to think of steam-powered vehicles while trudging home from church in the wake of a horse-drawn carriage. "What a noble thing it would be," he reportedly told himself, "if I could have such a carriage without the expense of keeping a horse." When a self-propelled steam carriage eluded Fitch, he turned to schemes for propelling boats with steam. In 1786, with a German partner, Fitch built a prototype that used steam to drive two rows of six oars on either side of the boat, connected by shafts and rigged to enter the water alternately, like the paddles of a canoe.

Fitch was just ahead of another American, James Rumsey, who in 1787 put a steam-powered boat into the Potomac River near Shepherdstown, Virginia. Simpler than Fitch's multipaddled design, the Rumsey boat used a kind of water-jet for propulsion, but it was less efficient and slower. Patents issued in 1791 shared credit between Rumsey and Fitch but described Rumsey's design, not Fitch's.

Part of Fitch's problem was a difficult personality and a terrible temper, which alienated potential supporters. Rumsey, on the other hand, was convincing, courteous, and unflappable. He was able to solicit generous help from Benjamin Franklin and other wealthy figures, and moved to England to build an improved steamboat, the *Columbian Maid.* As the craft neared completion in late 1792, however, Rumsey fell ill, and died on December 18. When the *Columbian Maid* finally sailed, she made only a poor four miles per hour.

Back in America, Fitch had put the eight-mile-per-hour *Thornton* to work on the Delaware in 1790 on a regular basis. By the fall of that year, the vessel had traveled some three thousand miles and carried a thousand passengers. But Fitch's success was merely technical. Economically, his steamboat could not compete with the stagecoach. This failure, the destruction in a storm of a new boat, and Fitch's realization that short-run steamboat routes could never prosper put an end to his increasingly desperate efforts.

Desolate, the luckless inventor moved to Bardstown, Kentucky, where he set out to drink himself to death, trading a bequest of 150 acres of nearby land to a tavern keeper for bed, board, and a pint of whiskey a day. When that failed to kill him, he increased the land bequest to double his whiskey ration. Finally, in 1798, he finished the job with opium pills.

Not until 1926 did Fitch receive any official credit for his steam-powered boats. It was in that year that the U.S. Congress appropriated $15,000 for a monument to the forgotten inventor at Bardstown. But Robert Fulton is forever called the father of the steamboat. □

In 1796, steamboat inventor John Fitch chose this idyllic setting on Collect Pond, located in present-day New York, for the trial run of an advanced design craft driven by a screw propeller.

Father of Invention

In 1791, fifteen years after he drafted America's Declaration of Independence and nine years before his tenure as the nation's third president, Thomas Jefferson wrote, "Science is my passion, politics my duty." He might have added that practical science—that is, invention—was the area where this passion was strongest.

The lord of the Virginia plantation called Monticello was fascinated by gadgets of any kind, and his interest was consumed by anything that saved time or labor.

In principle, Jefferson was opposed to the idea that anyone should win exclusive right to an invention: He deeply believed that so-called original ideas were really the product of collective achievements. Even so, he supervised the country's Patent Act of 1789. Although it ran against the grain of his convictions, the act shaped the foundations of the American patent system, which, as some historians have put it, "invented inventing." The first patent was issued on July 31, 1790, to Samuel Hopkins for "making pot and pearl ashes"—a cleaning formula called potash, then a key ingredient of soap.

Jefferson later noted that the law "has given a spring to invention beyond my conception." But, true to his principles, he never applied for protection for his inventions. Some of his designs were fairly simple: a folding campstool and a folding ladder, a portable copying desk. Others were mechanical. They included an innovative

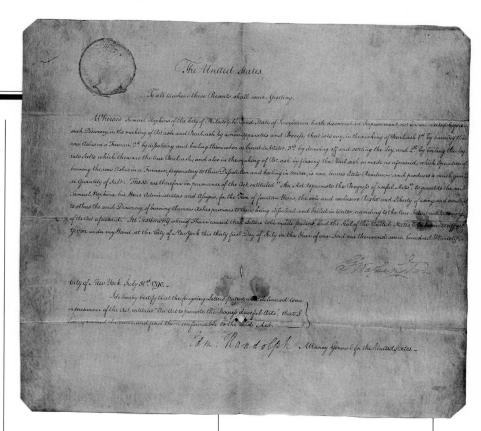

threshing machine and a plow that improved the efficiency with which the blade turned sod away from the furrow, making planting easier.

His most complex invention, however, was not a homely labor-saving device but an instrument of secrecy: a simple coding machine in which a series of lettered rings could be arranged to create practically unbreakable ciphers. He may well have used his homemade cipher wheel in the 1790s, while serving as George Washington's secretary of state. But the device, which might have revolutionized the diplomatic and military communications of his day, never entered widespread use.

More than a century later, U.S. Army cryptographers developed a cipher device called M-94, which used a series of rotating wheels on a common axis to generate codes. Developed as World War I began, the device became the standard army coding instrument in 1922. That same year, Jefferson's own description of the device came to light, and its modern creators realized that they had merely reinvented his wheel. □

Thomas Jefferson supervised the 1789 Patent Act, which permitted the first U.S. patent *(above)* to be issued in 1790, but he never patented his inventions, including a cipher wheel *(reconstructed below)* unknowingly reinvented by the army as World War I began.

Bitter Briton

The modern digital computer was not invented until the 1940s. Yet more than a century earlier, a cranky British mathematician named Charles Babbage designed and came close to building a mechanical computer out of screws, wires, levers, cams, and gears. Babbage's remarkable attempt was doomed, however, by its own complexity and a loss of confidence among his government backers. He died in 1871, convinced his life-work had failed.

In fact, the career of this bad-tempered banker's son should have been rich and fulfilling. Despite his cantankerous disposition, Babbage was one of London's most prominent socialites. His dinners, often for hundreds of guests, were famous, and he prided himself on friendships with John Stuart Mill; Charles Dickens; Alfred, Lord Tennyson; and other Victorian luminaries. Babbage was also a well-known locksmith, cryptographer, and inventor, credited with such widely varying designs as the first locomotive cowcatcher and the first actuarial tables for assessing life expectancy.

But his central fascination was with numbers. Sickly

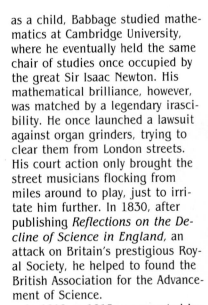

as a child, Babbage studied mathematics at Cambridge University, where he eventually held the same chair of studies once occupied by the great Sir Isaac Newton. His mathematical brilliance, however, was matched by a legendary irascibility. He once launched a lawsuit against organ grinders, trying to clear them from London streets. His court action only brought the street musicians flocking from miles around to play, just to irritate him further. In 1830, after publishing *Reflections on the Decline of Science in England,* an attack on Britain's prestigious Royal Society, he helped to found the British Association for the Advancement of Science.

In 1812 or 1813, exasperated by the poor quality of a series of French mathematical tables, Babbage embarked on the projects that would dominate his life. A machine, he reasoned, would eliminate the human error that had introduced the inaccuracies he had

British mathematician Charles Babbage *(above)* invented a complex calculating mechanism called the Difference Engine *(left)* in an attempt to out-compute the human brain.

seen. By 1822, he had made a rough prototype of what he called a Difference Engine, an intricate system of moving cams and gears. Although his scaled-down prototype worked, the full-size machine was too complex for the artisans of the period, who were unable to machine the carefully calibrated parts of a full-scale model.

The scheme drew the attention of the British government, which advanced Babbage £17,000 to continue research. Meanwhile, he had raised his sights from the Difference Engine to something he called the Analytical Engine. This machine, he said, would "move forward by biting its own tail"—instead of making single calculations, it would act as a computer, each step shaped by the results of the preceding calculations.

The design occupied him for almost forty years and grew progressively more complicated. Eventually, the plans for the machine required 50,000 separate parts, some produced at tolerances of tens of thousandths of an inch. (One of his mechanics was later knighted for learning to work to tolerances of millionths of an inch.)

Although more and more people threw up their hands at Babbage's grandiose invention, he retained one ardent supporter: Augusta Ada, countess of Lovelace, daughter of the poet Lord Byron and a brilliant mathematician. In Babbage's spare time, the pair devised a mathematical betting scheme for playing the horses. It was a disaster. The countess lost thousands of pounds and was pursued to her deathbed by irate bookmakers.

Babbage went to his own grave at seventy-eight an embittered man, his life clouded by the lack of recognition accorded his computing machine. Near the end, he told a friend that he could not remember a single happy day in his lifetime and that he hated organ grinders, the British government, and mankind. As to some future innovator taking up his work on an analytical engine, he had written earlier, "Half a century will probably elapse before anyone will attempt so unpromising a task."

Babbage was off but not by much. Seventy-three years after his death, the IBM automatic sequence controlled calculator, a computing machine that was startlingly similar to Babbage's proposed Analytical Engine, went into operation at Harvard University. □

Petite Pistol

The United States has been the birthplace of many of the world's deadliest and most admired firearms. A nineteenth-century Philadelphia gunsmith named Henry Deringer made many of them. In terms of popularity and notoriety, none of his weapons surpassed the compact, large-bore pistol he contrived around 1835 as a gentleman's defensive weapon. It was one of Deringer's models that John Wilkes Booth used thirty years later to assassinate Abraham Lincoln.

Born in Pennsylvania in 1786, Henry Deringer began selling guns as early as 1811, peddling muzzleloading squirrel rifles to Delaware boatmen and taking lumber in trade. In 1814, he landed the first of several contracts to sell rifles to the U.S. Army. The stubby, concealable pistol that he devised was largely notable for the size of its round bullet—forty to forty-five caliber—and rifling in its short barrel that made it superior to cheaper imitations. The little pistols were an instant hit and did much to make Deringer one of the biggest American armorers of his day.

But the stealthy handgun no longer bears its inventor's name—not quite anyway. European imitators, seeking to skirt U.S. patent law, began calling their wares "derringers," with a double r, and that was the name that finally stuck. □

Conceived by Henry Deringer as a gentleman's defensive weapon, the easily concealed pistol was also owned by villains. This one was used by John Wilkes Booth to assassinate Abraham Lincoln.

Joseph Henry used his early telegraph, shown here in replica, as a teaching aid long before Samuel Morse and others invented their telegraphic designs.

Induced Greatness

One of the greatest American scientist-inventors claimed that he was so indecisive that a cobbler had once resolved a dilemma for him by making a pair of shoes with one toe curved and the other square. But even with the defect of often being late to act, Joseph Henry helped bridge between the eighteenth-century electrical research of Benjamin Franklin *(page 10)* and the work of James Clerk Maxwell, who reduced electrodynamics to four equations in 1865.

Born in 1797, the son of an Albany, New York, drayman, Henry's boyhood interest in a theatrical career ended when, at sixteen, he discovered the world of science and invention. Apprenticed to a watchmaker and silversmith, the dreamy boy was found to be "too dull" for the work. After studying science in Albany, he began to teach there and became intrigued by the mysteries of electricity. It was known, for example, that an electrical current always generates a magnetic field of proportional

strength. Why, then, wondered Henry, couldn't a magnetic field generate electricity?

The answer he obtained in his laboratory was that varying magnetic fields do induce an electrical current in objects within the field. In 1830, Henry demonstrated electromagnetic induction, showing with simple equipment that magnetism and electricity can be converted into each other—the fundamental principle of electric communication and power generation.

Slow to publicize his finding, Henry lost credit for it when British physicist Michael Faraday published an account of his own discovery of induction in 1831. But Henry went on. During the years at Albany, and later at what is now Princeton University, he invented the world's most powerful electromagnets, an electric motor, and, years before Charles Wheatstone, William Fothergill Cooke, and Samuel Morse, built a simple version of the telegraph.

Henry sought no patent for that

or any of his other inventions. He thought it incompatible "with the dignity of science to confine benefits which might be derived from it to the exclusive use of any individual." But, perhaps recalling his loss to Faraday, he added, "In this, I was perhaps too fastidious." With characteristic generosity, Henry later supported Morse's bid for government aid to build the country's first telegraph line.

In 1846, he was selected as the first secretary of the new Smithsonian Institution. There, he created the forerunner of the U.S. Weather Service, pioneered sunspot research, and used his enormous influence in the advancement of science. Still, until his death in 1878, Henry nursed some regret that he had not published before Faraday and thus gained recognition for his landmark discovery. Credit came posthumously: In 1893, the International Electrical Congress decreed that the scientific unit for measuring inductance would be known as the henry. □

By Gum!

The notion that inventors are driven individuals, single-mindedly sacrificing family and friends to an elusive idea, owes much to obsessive questers such as Charles Goodyear. Although the central discovery of his career was sparked by an accident, he had approached that moment by living, breathing, dreaming, and wearing rubber, the material that obsessed him, for five impoverished years.

But crushing debt was the norm for Goodyear. Like his father, a Connecticut hardware dealer and inventor in his own right, Charles was an abysmal businessman. The twenty-six-year-old entrepreneur opened his own store in Philadelphia in 1826, enjoyed a mildly prosperous interval, and, probably through mismanagement, went suddenly bankrupt. He became a blacksmith but could not climb out of debt. In 1829, he endured the first of many humiliating sentences in debtor's prison.

Goodyear's obsession with the elastic gum extracted from the rubber tree began in 1834. While tinkering with the valve of a rubberized life preserver, Goodyear was struck by the substance's unusual properties.

In its natural form, rubber lacks the firm, resilient qualities of today's commercial product. It coagulates from a milky sap into a solid soon after extraction from the tree. In Goodyear's time, this solid was liquefied with such solvents as turpentine to form a material that melted in relatively low heat, cracked in the cold, and decomposed after exposure to air and light. Early pioneers had found ways to sandwich the sticky substance between layers of canvas to fashion crude waterproof garments. But efforts to form rubber into objects such as boots had produced nothing but failure.

Immediately intrigued by the peculiar material, the thirty-four-year-old inventor believed that a fortune could be made if rubber's consistency could be stabilized. He began boiling, steaming, and mixing the substance to achieve that result and nearly asphyxiated himself in one chemical experiment. Goodyear also took to wearing rubber clothing and shoes on the streets of New York, much to the amusement of friends.

But Goodyear's mania was no joke to his family, who often went hungry as the would-be inventor struggled on, supported only by what he could pawn or sell. At times, the family had to beg for food. By 1839, Goodyear had almost reached the end of his tether. After moving to Woburn, Massachusetts, he had entered into partnership with the owner of a failed rubber company and, with the backing of a businessman, was chasing one illusory breakthrough after another. With each failure, Goodyear's credibility and fortunes continued to sink.

One day in 1839, while heating a concoction of rubber, sulfur, and white lead, Goodyear accidentally dropped some onto the stove, charring but not melting it. Suddenly, he had his miracle: The surviving rubber had the elastic stability he had sought for so long. Still, it took five more years for Goodyear to develop his process to a point where he felt secure ◊

Charles Goodyear dedicated much of his life to perfecting a recipe for rubber, then spent a fortune creating rubber paraphernalia like those shown below.

enough to seek a patent for it. His family continued to suffer. At one point, he pawned the children's schoolbooks to continue work. His young son, perhaps weakened by a meager diet, fell ill and died. And even with success in view, Goodyear could not escape the occasional trip to debtor's prison.

Greedy competitors continually usurped his claims. British manufacturer Thomas Hancock, who had tried for years to achieve what Goodyear had, deftly picked up samples of Goodyear's rubber, analyzed it, and gave the process the name it bears today: vulcanization, for Vulcan, Roman god of fire.

Meanwhile, Goodyear poured the growing income from his invention into new experiments and a flood of objects that could use his new substance: tents, squeegee mops, conveyor belts. In 1851, at the famed Crystal Palace exhibition in London, he created the bizarre Vulcanite Court, a huge room covered in rubber sheets and filled with rubber objects. The cost was enormous for the day: $30,000. He won a medal, but his debts continued to mount. In 1855, he won more honors at a Paris exhibition—his son handed them to Goodyear in a Paris debtor's prison. Emperor Napoleon III later

visited Goodyear at a hotel to express his admiration.

The secret of Goodyear's rubber process was popular game for patent pirates, and he had to fight hard in court to protect his rights. At one point, he hired Secretary of State Daniel Webster to defend his patent. When Goodyear died in 1860—possibly of lead poisoning—he left behind hundreds of thousands of dollars in debts. Although the government refused to renew his patent in the name of his heirs, his sons, apparently armed with the commercial ingenuity Goodyear lacked, were finally able to make the family rich. □

Grim Reaper

In 1834, Cyrus McCormick, later famed as the inventor of the revolutionary mechanical grain reaper, was reading *Mechanics Magazine* and came upon a picture of another reaper invented by one Obed Hussey and patented in 1833. He quickly wrote to the publication, noting that the Hussey device incorporated principles McCormick had used in a reaper of his own design. His warning against "further infringement" of his as yet unpatented invention became the first shot in the contest known as the reaper war.

Hussey had never heard of McCormick, however, or of any reaper but his own. A scrupulously honest Quaker, he was the gentlest of men—despite a piratical patch over his left eye, the result of an injury received during Hussey's youth. He was

also an inventor of some note, having designed various grinding and husking machines before he launched his search for the key to the dauntingly complicated reaper. Hussey eventually produced a horse-drawn carriage with a long knife of triangular steel teeth that cut back and forth as the machine moved forward and did the work of as many as six laborers.

When Hussey patented his reap-

er, McCormick was still tinkering with his own model. But a decade later, the rival reapers were competing fiercely in demonstration contests around the country—and even in England—to see which was better. Overall, their performances were about the same. Hussey had considerable support in Congress for his primacy over the McCormick invention but was finally thwarted by the government's decision that the reaper was too important to be monopolized by a single man. The reaper war was really won, however, by McCormick's marketing genius. While Hussey concentrated his sales efforts in the East, McCormick moved his operations to Chicago, where his salesmen could sell reapers to the expanding midwestern breadbasket.

Hussey's business dwindled; he sold it in 1858. "I made no money during the existence of my patent," he wrote a friend. "No

Although history gives Cyrus McCormick credit for inventing the reaper, another contemporary design (*left*) was developed by Obed Hussey (*above*), a gentle and scrupulously honest man rendered sinister looking by an eye patch.

man knows how much I have suffered in body and mind since 1833, on account of this thing." Two years later, Hussey was dead, a victim not of the reaper wars but of his unflagging kindness. A little girl on the Boston-Portland train asked him for a drink of water. The sixty-eight-year-old inventor graciously went into the station to fetch her one and, trying to reboard the train as it got under way, slipped beneath its wheels and was killed. □

Creative Communists

Inventive genius is individual almost by definition. But every so often, a shared spark of creativity flares into life among a community of innovators. The Shakers, a religious sect that began in Manchester, England, in the eighteenth century, were one of these rare collectives. (Their name was bestowed upon the Shakers because of the whirling, jerking ecstasy of their religious services.)

Shakerism was founded by Ann Lee, an illiterate British factory worker and blacksmith's daughter. Mother Ann, as she came to be known, was inspired by a doctrine of labor and simplicity. "Put your hands to work and your hearts to God," was one of her maxims. She believed that her followers should forswear sex and private property, live in communal surroundings, and dedicate themselves to salvation through work. Mother Ann and her followers were opposed to capitalism but had a keen interest in technology: Anything that improved productivity of labor, they felt, must be divinely inspired.

Viewed askance by the rising capitalistic class of Britain's industrial revolution, Shakerism moved to America. Mother Ann and eight followers set sail in 1774 for New York, where her gospel found fertile soil in the hardworking colonies. The religion was formally established in 1787. By 1840, when Shakerism was at its height, there were 6,000 believers living in nineteen communal villages spread from New England to Kentucky.

For Shakers, God lay in the details of their work and the quality of their artisanship; they took great pride in, and care with, both. Nowadays, they are remembered best for the exquisitely plain furniture and implements that filled their dwellings and for the rib-knit design of Shaker sweaters. But innovation, as well as simplicity, was one of their watchwords. Among the devices they created were the apple corer, an early threshing machine, and a pioneering form of wash-and-wear cloth.

Shakers invented a planing machine, a turbine waterwheel, a revolving oven, a fertilizing machine, and an apparatus for reeling silk thread. Shaker David Parker, of Canterbury, New Hampshire, is considered the possible inventor of the first washing machine, which used a combination of steam and waterjets to clean clothes. The circular saw was invented by a female Shaker, one Sister Tabitha, who felt that using a straight or curved variety amounted to a waste of time. Neither she nor most other members of the sect patented their hundreds of inventions.

By the end of the American Civil War, the Shakers had begun to dwindle away, doomed by their refusal to reproduce themselves. Their celibate status meant their collective survival depended on recruitment or adoption of new members. Both of those measures were easier in a rural setting, and the United States was rapidly becoming a society of towns and cities. By the late 1800s, the group had ceased to hold public meetings for lack of adequate membership. In 1974, when a group called Friends of the Shakers held a bicentennial celebration of the sect's arrival in the New World, only two communes remained, one in Sabbathday Lake, Maine, and the other in Canterbury, New Hampshire, both of them still active today. □

The Shakers, a religious group known for its innovations, invented a host of practical devices, including the circular saw shown at left.

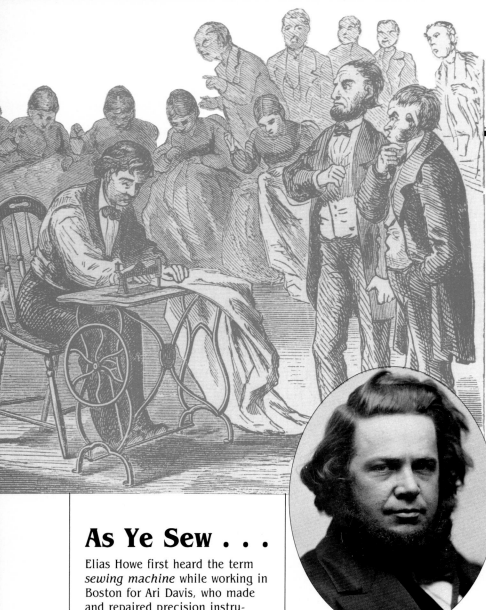

As Ye Sew . . .

Elias Howe first heard the term *sewing machine* while working in Boston for Ari Davis, who made and repaired precision instruments. People had been trying to invent such a device for half a century in America and abroad, without any great success. Some early devices patented in England simply did not work. A functional sewing machine, introduced by French tailor Barthélemy Thimonnier in 1830, roused tailors to radical action. Fearing that they would be put out of business by the labor-saving equipment, they stormed and destroyed Thimonnier's eighty-machine plant. The inventor fled and later died a bankrupt. In 1834, Walter Hunt, credited with creating a forerunner of the Winchester re-peating rifle and the safety pin, built America's first sewing machine but lost interest in a device he saw as a destroyer of jobs. But Ari Davis thought such a machine would make someone a fortune, and Howe took his employer's opinions to heart.

Born in 1819 in Spencer, Massachusetts, Howe had apprenticed to a textile mill at sixteen, then, unemployed after the panic of 1837, moved to the big city to seek work and apprenticed to Davis. By the early 1840s, he had married and had children to support. But Howe, always in frail health, became too ill to work. His wife began to take in sewing to pay the growing family's bills. Watching her at work, Howe realized that no machine would be able to duplicate the motions of hand and arm in sewing. Instead, he hit on a process that used thread from two different sources. A needle with its eye at the point would push through the cloth, creating a loop of thread on the far side; then a shuttle would slip thread through the loop, creating a tight lock stitch.

As he began to build his device, misfortune dogged him. His workshop burned down, and his machines turned out to cost some $300 each, far more than most households could afford. In an 1845 demonstration, his invention out-sewed five seamstresses, but he was unable to sell a single machine. Armed with an 1846 patent, he tried to promote sales of the device in England but was swindled out of his British royalties. Then, unemployed and desperate, Howe accepted a meager three pounds a week offered by the swindler to improve the pirated design. Once that had been achieved, however, Howe was fired. He managed to ship his family home, then pawned his patent model and papers to buy his own passage back to America. Soon after his return to Boston, his loyal wife died.

The sewing-machine business, however, was flourishing. Howe found that in his absence other inventors had usurped his discovery and sewing machines of various designs were everywhere in use. The most successful was that of Isaac Singer, who combined mechanical talent with the marketing flair that Howe lacked. Singer's sewing machine differed from Howe's: Its needle moved up and down, rather than sideways, and it was powered by a treadle rather than a hand crank. But it used the same lock stitch process and a similar needle.

Funded by a mortgage on his father's farm, Howe went to court and began to sue the infringers. After years of legal battles, his patent was upheld in 1854, and Singer was ordered to pay fifteen thousand dollars in back royalties. When the various manufacturers pooled their patents in 1856, Howe managed to negotiate a five-dollar royalty for each machine sold in the United States and one dollar for each sold abroad. The deal brought him two million dollars, the wealth he had dreamed of years before. But the struggle had taken its toll, and the forty-eight-year-old Howe died in 1867, the year his patent expired. □

Inventive Abe

One of the more obscure memorials to Abraham Lincoln lies in the files of the U.S. Patent Office. On May 22, 1849—twelve years before he took office as the sixteenth American president—"Honest Abe" won a patent for a device to help steamboats pass over shoals and sand bars.

Lincoln's device consisted of a set of adjustable buoyancy chambers, made of metal and water-proof cloth attached to the ship just below the water line. Slung from the sides of ships on vertical shafts, they could be raised or lowered as necessary. Bellows would be used to fill the chambers with air, and they would float the vessel to safety. The design was never manufactured or, as far as is known, even tested. But it remains distinctive as the only patent ever held by a U.S. president. □

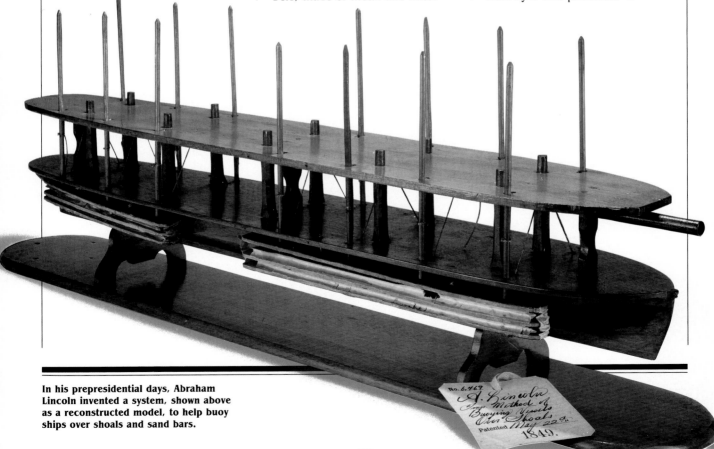

In his prepresidential days, Abraham Lincoln invented a system, shown above as a reconstructed model, to help buoy ships over shoals and sand bars.

Lamp of Knowledge

"A chemist who is not a physicist is nothing," proclaimed Robert Bunsen, the German inventor-chemist whose name, attached to the burner he perfected, is familiar in every high-school science laboratory. But his inventive genius was chiefly an accessory to his lifework as a brilliant chemist.

Born in Göttingen in 1811, Bunsen had a strong interest in the chemistry underlying industrial processes, which he helped make more efficient. After winning renown for his work in analytical chemistry, Bunsen turned to a study of organic arsenic compounds and discovered that hydrated ferric oxide could be administered as an antidote for arsenic poisoning. Bunsen made many of his own instruments, including the famed burner, which mixes air and gas to produce a hot, smokeless, nonluminous flame for heating chemical compounds.

Working with German physicist Gustav Kirchhoff, Bunsen combined his burner with the optical system developed by Joseph von Fraunhofer, to study the properties of chemicals, founding the science of spectroscopy in the process. When substances are heated until they glow, they produce a distinctive rainbowlike spectrum, each with its own unique patterns of colors and lines. Bunsen discovered two new elements with the technique: cesium and rubidium.

The famous burner is not all that bears his name. Bunsen also is credited with an improved battery, the Bunsen cell, and a nickel compound, bunsenite, was named in his honor. □

The smokeless, nonluminous gas burner *(above)* used by chemistry students was named for its inventor, German Robert Bunsen *(left)*.

Dynamite Fellow

Alfred Bernhard Nobel, the man who invented the world's most commonly used explosive, was a lifelong bachelor, a stickler for etiquette, and a brooding literary figure who called himself a "wreck on the sea of life." Although his chemical inventions brought him vast wealth and reputation, he found little happiness.

Chemistry and invention were in Nobel's blood from birth. He was born in Stockholm in 1833, the fourth son of Immanuel Nobel, an inventor whose life was a roller coaster of alternating failure and success. In 1842, the family moved to St. Petersburg, where the senior Nobel was building sea mines and other weapons for Russia. The Nobels remained there until the late 1850s, when a new Russian government canceled their contracts. While the family was still in Russia, Alfred often left to travel and extend his considerable talent for language. In Paris, he became a chemist of notable ability, and his first patent was issued in 1857, when Nobel was twenty-four.

His father had used gunpowder in his sea mines but had always hoped for something more powerful. In 1846, an Italian chemist, Ascanio Sobrero, discovered that mixing glycerol with nitric and sulfuric acids produced a yellowish, oily substance with astonishing explosive power. Sobrero decided his invention was too unpredictable to be put to use. But Immanuel Nobel began to toy with it as a substitute for gunpowder.

The problem was that the volatile liquid—known as nitroglycer-

Alfred Nobel found nitroglycerin could be mixed with clay to form a stable explosive—dynamite (being made at left in an 1800s New Jersey plant).

in—could be detonated only by a shock, and no one had found a way to do this at a distance. But Alfred had an answer. Only a few months after rejoining his father in Stockholm in 1863, Nobel had invented the blasting cap—a fuzed gunpowder (later, fulminate of mercury) charge that could be used to detonate an adjacent explosive.

But even with the detonators, liquid nitroglycerin remained dangerously and unpredictably unstable. In September 1864, it caused the Nobels' detonator factory at nearby Heleneborg to explode, killing the youngest Nobel brother, Oscar Emil, and four others. The death of his son caused Immanuel to have a stroke from which he never fully recovered. Worldwide, scores of people were killed while manufacturing, shipping, or using the dangerous substance.

Meanwhile, Alfred hit on the idea of mixing the oily liquid with some kind of porous material that would take away its deadly instability and that could be safely transported and molded. He found the right combination by blending about 75 percent nitroglycerin with 25 percent of a common sediment called kieselguhr, which is absorbent, chemically neutral, and abundant. The resulting explosive was much more powerful than gunpow-

der and only slightly less potent than nitroglycerin. Nobel named it dynamite, after *dynamis,* the Greek word for "power."

Dynamite made Nobel immensely wealthy, and he went on to make many other inventions, including a form of smokeless gunpowder. But he was never really happy and led a rootless existence that inspired author Victor Hugo to call him the millionaire vagabond. An occasional writer of novels, plays, and poems, Nobel was always a pacifist. He once told a like-minded friend that his factories might do more for peace than all her pacifist congresses "because the day that two armies have the capacity to annihilate each other within a few seconds, it is then likely that all civilized nations will turn their backs on warfare." Thus, he was jolted in 1888 when, upon his brother Ludvig's death, a newspaper printed Alfred's obituary by mistake—and labeled him the Merchant of Death.

The insult deepened his interest in pacifism and in establishing a memorial beyond his deadly innovations. He prepared a will directing that most of his fortune of about nine million dollars—an immense sum then—be used to

give prizes in literature, chemistry, physics, physiology or medicine, and peace (economics was added in 1968) to "those persons who shall have contributed most materially to benefit mankind."

Never robust, Nobel developed a serious heart condition in the 1890s. Living at his Italian villa in San Remo in the fall of 1896, he had a cerebral hemorrhage that destroyed his ability to speak anything but his native Swedish, and that only haltingly. A servant found him dead on December 10. Nobel had succumbed despite treatment with a sweet-tasting medication: nitroglycerin, used to dilate the blood vessels of heart patients. □

Reaching Out

The sound of human voices shaped the family life of young Alexander Graham Bell, the inventor of the telephone. His grandfather was a well-known Scottish lecturer, his father a teacher of linguistics and the inventor of what he called visible speech, a phonetic language derived from the positions of the tongue, lips, and throat as they formed various sounds.

At one point, young Alexander wanted to be a concert pianist, but at sixteen, he became a teacher of elocution and music, then studied to help his father perfect the phonetic language. Perhaps because his mother's hearing was seriously impaired, he also had an abiding interest in deafness, a common affliction of the day, and began experiments that used visible speech to help deaf children learn to speak. In 1870, after two of Alexander's brothers succumbed to tuberculosis, the Bells moved to Canada. By then, Alexander had become a speech instructor of the deaf and soon went to Boston to teach. In 1872, he opened his own school for training teachers of the deaf and, a year later, became a professor of vocal physiology at newly created Boston University.

In Boston, he became fascinated by telegraphy, and early experiments convinced him that the instrument should be able to do more than send one message at a time over a strand of wire. He wanted to invent a device capable of sending many messages at once, much as a musical chord carries multiple notes. Bell began to work on his "harmonic telegraph."

As it happened, one of his students was a deaf woman named

Mabel Hubbard, whose financier father, Gardiner Hubbard, had an aggressive interest in telegraphy. Aided by Hubbard, the twenty-seven-year-old inventor soon had access to a lab and a full-time assistant named Thomas Watson.

In 1874, Bell realized that a metal plate vibrating at a particular pitch of sound could transmit those same vibrations to another plate through an electrical circuit. Sound vibrations, he saw, could be transformed into corresponding undulations in an electrical current, then converted back into sound. His breakthrough came by accident. His multiple telegraph used metal reeds to create its complicated tones. One day his assistant secured a reed too tightly to its electrical contact and plucked it. Bell, listening at the

Telephone inventor Alexander Graham Bell became a mentor for many young people struggling with deafness, among them Helen Keller *(above, left)*, shown with Bell and the great teacher he recommended, Anne Sullivan.

circuit in another room, heard the twang. He rushed out, shouting, "Don't change a thing!"

Finally, on March 7, 1876, after refining the basic apparatus, Bell was granted U.S. patent number 174,465, the fundamental patent for the telephone. Three days later, at his Boston laboratory, Bell placed the epoch-making first phone call to his assistant in the next room. "Mr. Watson," he said, "come here. I want to see you." He obtained a second basic patent in early 1877. And on July 9 of that year, Bell, Hubbard, and Thomas Sanders, the father of a former pupil, founded the Bell Telephone Company. Two days later, Alexander and Mabel were married.

Bell's 1876 patent is often called the most valuable in history. It was Bell's partners, however, who made the Bell Telephone Company a huge success. The inventor of the telephone gave most of his 30 percent share in the firm to Mabel as a wedding present and, in 1881, retired from the business.

For the rest of his life, Bell exercised his wide-ranging interest in almost everything. Fascinated by flight, he experimented with manned kites. In 1880, he conceived of a "photophone," which would transmit speech by a long beam of light, using a selenium receptor. After an infant son died, Bell created a form of iron lung, dubbed a vacuum jacket. When President James Garfield was shot in 1881, Bell invented an electric probe that could find embedded bullets. Garfield's wounds killed him before the device was perfected, but it was in common use by hospitals in the days before medical x-rays. Bell even dabbled with the electrical aspects of extrasensory perception: He would coil wire around his head and that of an assistant to see if thoughts would leap the gap. By the early 1900s, Bell had begun building hydrofoil speedboats, and in 1919, one of his designs set a world speed record of seventy miles per hour.

As the tall, methodical Scot became the portly, bearded philanthropist, he steadfastly tried to communicate his own great enthusiasm for science and discovery. He financed the American journal *Science* for twelve years and was an important force behind creation of the National Geographic Soci-

ety and its monthly magazine, whose first editor married one of Bell's daughters.

For all his achievements in sending the human voice across great distances, however, he was to the end of his life sharply aware that many people still spent their lives locked in silence. His most

famous protégée was Helen Keller, left deaf and blind by a childhood illness, who dedicated her autobiography to the great teacher of the deaf. "He is never quite so happy," she wrote, "as when he has a little deaf child in his arms." And Bell himself always listed his occupation as teacher of the deaf. □

Lady Edison

Big, strong, and soft-voiced, Margaret "Mattie" Knight was not like other girls her age in mid-nineteenth-century New England. Born in 1838, she created her first invention at age twelve, a cutoff device that shut down a power-loom automatically when a steel-tipped shuttle fell out.

Young Mattie never patented that creation and did not obtain her first patent until twenty years later, in 1870, when she invented an improved machine to make paper bags with flat bottoms instead of the usual V-shaped ones. She later held patents on shoe-cutting machines and even invented a new

valve sleeve for an auto engine.

Largely self-taught, Mattie Knight was dubbed Lady Edison for her fertile mechanical mind and her eventual twenty-seven patents. She never married, and her creativity never made her rich. When she died in 1914, her entire estate was valued at only $275.05. As a self-supporting working-class woman, she had rarely been able to wait for royalties but sold the rights to her inventions outright. □

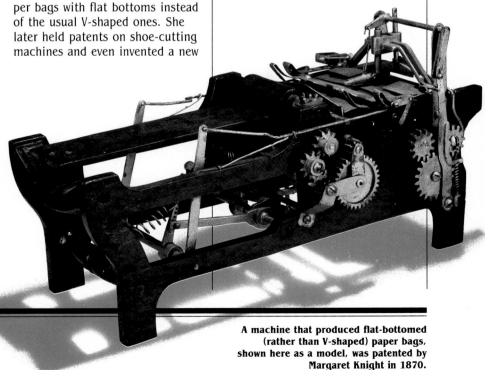

A machine that produced flat-bottomed (rather than V-shaped) paper bags, shown here as a model, was patented by Margaret Knight in 1870.

So Vain

Jules Léotard *(left)* was born in France in 1842 and, by his own account, had to be hung upside down from a trapeze to stop his crying as a child. That, and many other claims, are made in his *Memoirs,* written after Léotard, who perfected the aerial somersault, had become one of France's most famous aerialists. His autobiography also lauds one of his fashion creations, a one-piece, sleeveless, elastic garment invented for his trapeze act but pitched to male vanity. "Do you want to be adored by the ladies?" the conceited acrobat asked his readers. Then "put on a more natural garb, which does not hide your best features." Eventually, his trapeze clothes were sewn to include arms. To this day, they remain the basic uniform of circus performers and dancers. □

Riveting Design

The most popular trousers in the world are named after a quiet, industrious San Francisco dry-goods merchant, even though they were invented by someone else.

Levi Strauss was a German-born merchant's son who came to America in 1847. He became a peddler, tramping eastern back roads with a pack of pots, pans, duck cloth, and sewing supplies. In 1852, he sailed to San Francisco to join his brother-in-law in cashing in on the gold rush. Other Strauss family members helped the two men open a dry-goods store selling hats, shirts, and canvas. Within a decade their firm, Levi Strauss & Company, was one of San Francisco's most prosperous dry-goods outlets.

One day in 1872, the partners got a letter from a Reno, Nevada, tailor by the name of Jacob Davis. A Latvian immigrant who had changed his name from Jacob Youphes, Davis plied his trade with Levi Strauss cloth, mainly for miners at the nearby Comstock lode. Two years earlier, he had made an extrastrong pair of duck-twill trousers for a local woodcutter and had been inspired to fasten the pockets with copper rivets to fight wear and tear. The riveted pants were a mounting success, and Davis was worried.

"My nabors are getting yealouse of these success and unless I secure it by Patent Papers it will soon become a general thing," he wrote. Davis lacked the necessary money either to protect or exploit his idea by himself. He asked the Strauss family to join him in patenting the design and taking on

THE HORSEMAN'S FAVORITE GARMENTS

LEVI STRAUSS & CO.
PATENT-RIVETED CLOTHING
SAN FRANCISCO, CAL.

manufacture and distribution. Levi Strauss agreed and, after some tinkering, won a patent in 1873. Davis became the company's production supervisor.

The new trousers quickly attracted a booming working-class clientele. The Levi Strauss company made two varieties of trousers: heavy blue denim pants—the color was reliable, cheap, and hid stains—that they described by its lot number, 501, and an off-white, duck-twill style of cloth that had originally been made in Genoa. Both types of cloth derived their names from the French: *Denim* came from *serge de Nîmes,* a cloth made in that city; and because Genoa is Gene in French, the twill pants were called *jeans.*

Strauss became an extremely wealthy man and devoted more and more of his attention to philanthropy. When he died in 1902, flags in San Francisco's wholesale district were flown at half-mast, and stores were closed in his memory. The pants that made him rich and famous have endured almost as Davis first designed them, with minor changes. The rear pocket rivets were sheathed in 1937 to prevent scratching of chairs and saddles, and vanished completely during the 1960s. And modern Levi's are missing the original crotch rivet, which became too hot for comfort if the wearer stood near a fire. □

Miners, woodcutters, and cowboys out West, like the horseman pictured above in an early ad, wore the durable, copper-riveted pants sold by Levi Strauss *(right)* long before Easterners adopted them as high fashion.

Eccentric Émigré

Perhaps the most dramatic inventor of the modern age was Nikola Tesla, an intellectual giant who bested Thomas Edison and Guglielmo Marconi at their own specialties—but died an obscure recluse. Tesla was, as one admiring scientist put it, "so far ahead of his time that the rest of us then mistook him for a dreamer." He was also a scientific cult figure: Some enthusiasts believed he had come to Earth from Venus, and many thought him the inventor of a mysterious death ray.

Tesla's greatest invention was the alternating-current, or ac, motor, the central element of all the world's electrical power systems. It permits the transmission of the high-voltage current that makes long-distance power transmission—and almost all household appliances—possible. He also invented the Tesla coil, which converts low-voltage electricity into a high-voltage spark.

But Tesla's talents ranged far beyond electrical power. He produced prototypes of the radio transmitter, fluorescent lighting, and radio-controlled robots, as well as a forerunner to the electron microscope. Long before cosmic rays were discovered, Tesla speculated on their existence.

Tesla, a clergyman's son, was born in 1856 in Smiljan in what is now Yugoslavia. A sickly child, he suffered from apparitions that took the form of flashes of light. He had a photographic memory, and as his apparitions became less frequent, he acquired an uncanny ability to visualize mechanical devices precisely, without drawing them. His inventions came to him fully formed. After studying electrical engineering in Austria, Tesla went to work for a Hungarian telegraph company. His alternating-current discovery came when he was twenty-five. Strolling with a friend in a Budapest park, Tesla was reciting poetry when suddenly he fell into a trance. When he emerged, he sketched an alternating-current electrical motor in the dirt. Essentially, it used changing magnetic fields to turn a rotor. There were almost no moving parts.

In 1884, Tesla moved to America and worked for Edison. He soon quit, claiming that his boss had cheated him out of a $50,000 bonus for improving Edison direct-current dynamos. More important, perhaps, Edison rejected Tesla's alternating-current idea, despite its practical advantages: It could be generated at high voltages and efficiently transmitted over long distances, and its voltage stepped down with transformers to provide both alternating and direct current.

The émigré inventor found a backer in George Westinghouse and sold the financier rights to his ac creation for $70,000, plus a princely $2.50 for every horsepower of electricity generated. His huge stake in direct current threatened, Edison claimed alternating current was deadly, and one of his employees arranged that a Westinghouse generator be installed to power New York State's electric chair; the Edison camp even suggested that death by electrocution be called

A death mask *(above)* preserves the countenance of Nikola Tesla, a remarkable, eccentric inventor who achieved fame and fortune when he pioneered such fields as alternating-current electricity, radio transmission, and robots. Despite early glory, Tesla died an impoverished recluse.

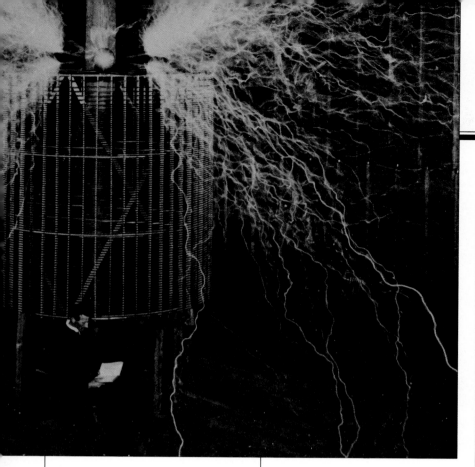

Westinghousing. Tesla helped lay such anti-ac rumors to rest by lighting a wireless lamp with alternating current passed through his body. But the obvious benefits of alternating current won the day. Eventually, Westinghouse won the contract to illuminate the 1893 Chicago World's Fair and, three years later, the contract to harness Niagara Falls to produce electricity. Tesla's system had won out.

His royalty arrangement should have made him a billionaire, but Tesla's own eccentric nature prevailed. Westinghouse ran into financial trouble, and bankers refused to help unless he got out of the deal with Tesla. When the financier took that ultimatum to the inventor, Tesla accepted a cash settlement of $216,600.

By then the world had become accustomed to Tesla's quirks. He hobnobbed with high-flying financiers and lived at New York's Waldorf-Astoria Hotel, where his eccentricities were legion. He was afraid to be near women wearing pearl earrings and would not shake hands for fear of germs. Before eating, he calculated the volume of each dish and polished his silverware at each meal with eighteen linen napkins—eighteen because he favored numbers divisible by three. Tesla was also a compulsive showman. He aired all ideas, brilliant or half-baked, in the press rather than in scientific journals. His Manhattan laboratory was a technological circus where giant Tesla coils threw off huge sparks, and the inventor lit electric lights by holding them in his hands while he stood in high-voltage electrical fields. In 1898, he appeared at Madison Square Garden to show off a three-foot boat that maneuvered by radio commands. It was a forerunner, he said, of "teleautomatics"—intelligent robots that would do the work of the future.

These early triumphs made it easy for Tesla to raise money for further experiments from plutocrats such as J. P. Morgan. In 1899, Tesla built an experimental center in Colorado Springs to study high-voltage electrical transmission without wires: man-made lightning. He threw sparks 135 feet into the air and blew out the local power supply. He decided that a similar immense transmitter could beam radio waves to Europe and convinced Morgan to finance a towering facility on Long Island. But Morgan supplied only a fraction of the money required and the facility was never completed.

In 1901, a simpler transmitter invented by the Italian Guglielmo Marconi sent radio signals across the Atlantic. At the time, a friend remarked to Tesla, "Looks like Marconi got the jump on you."

"Marconi is a good fellow," Tesla replied. "Let him continue. He is using seventeen of my patents." In the event, however, Tesla received little recognition for his pioneering radio work. In 1915, he sued Marconi for infringement of a radio patent and the court ruled in his favor. But he never won the popular credit he was due.

The inventor's reputation began to decline as his interests grew steadily less practical. When he made down-to-earth breakthroughs, he did not bother to patent them. Slowly, his grandiose lifestyle faded. He became reclusive, walking the city at night, feeding pigeons. The eighty-seven-year-old visionary was surrounded by birds when he died in his sleep in 1943—the same year that the Supreme Court ruled once more that he, not the rich and famous Marconi, had invented the first radio-wave transmitter. □

The Wiz

No one has captured the essence of American inventiveness quite so well as Thomas Alva Edison, the folksy and self-taught father of electric lighting, the phonograph, the mimeograph machine, the fluoroscope, the electric typewriter, and hundreds of other familiar, everyday objects.

His impulse for innovation never rested, and no idea was too large or small for Edison to try. After producing his great creation, the carbon-filament light bulb, for example, he perfected power generators, electrical meters, power switches, power lines, voltage regulators, and insulated wire—the full set of components used in an electrical power system.

It took Edison only eighteen months to invent his light bulb, and he joked that "we will make electric light so cheap that only the rich will be able to burn candles." In all, he amassed 1,093 patents—far more than any other American inventor before or since.

But Edison had his dark side. He was arrogant, abrasive, and bullheaded—and not above pirating ideas or slandering competitors' products. But he so effectively manipulated the press to create his image as a godlike genius of American industry that one assistant ranked him with the circus impresario P. T. Barnum. In fact, Edison sank millions of dollars into wasteful and ill-considered industrial schemes. His antisubmarine devices for the U.S. Navy, for example, were ignored as useless. Even Edison's vaunted electrical power system had a fatal weakness: It was limited by his stubborn reliance on direct current, which could not be transmitted over distances of much more than a mile without severe power losses.

Edison was born in Milan, Ohio, in 1847, the youngest of seven children. He dropped out of grammar school after only three months but continued to read voraciously, especially after scarlet fever left him progressively deaf from the age of twelve. By then he had already begun tinkering with electricity and chemistry.

When he was sixteen, Edison became a roving telegraph operator. His first patent soon followed: a design for a telegraphic vote-recording machine. No one was interested. At twenty-one, he had his first commercial success, an improved telegraphic stock ticker. He began manufacturing the machine and filed forty-six patents over the years for improvements to it. Such attention to detail lay behind his famous observation that invention is "99 percent perspiration and 1 percent inspiration."

Patents continued to roll out of his workshop in Newark, New Jersey, where he had settled in 1870. He was granted thirty-eight patents in 1872, when he was twenty-five, and he got twenty-five more the next year. In 1874, he invented a telegraph that would send up to four messages at a time, a device similar to one Alexander Graham Bell abandoned on his road to the telephone *(page 26)*.

In 1876, Edison left Newark for a new complex at nearby Menlo Park, where he promised "a minor invention every ten days, and a big thing every six months or so." In effect, the establishment at Menlo Park was also an invention: the modern industrial research laboratory, in which needs were identified and inventions developed to fill them. Edison soon kept his promise. While investigating the limits of Bell's telephone patents, Edison hit on the carbon transmitter that became standard in the machine. His phonograph was another bit of inspired luck: Edison was actually seeking a way to record telegraph signals.

In 1878, with the backing of millionaires J. P. Morgan and Cornelius Vanderbilt, the Wizard of Menlo Park—as Edison had been dubbed by admiring writers—launched his epic quest for a workable electric light bulb. His painstaking discovery of carbonized thread as the proper filament is part of folklore.

But Edison was after more than a mere light bulb: He wanted to illuminate entire cities. He had concluded that a citywide home lighting system was only possible if bulbs offered high resistance to electrical current, and carbon did that job best.

Edison's first wife died in 1884. By then, he was a folk hero: When Menlo Park opened to visitors, special trains had to be scheduled to handle the traffic. Remarried in 1886, Edison moved with his bride to West Orange, New Jersey, where the couple lived in baronial splendor befitting his growing vision of himself as a manufacturing tycoon. He was not cut out for such a grandiose role, however. His scheme to build prefabricated concrete houses complete with ready-made concrete furniture came to nothing. A failed search for ways to refine low-grade metallic ore through magnetism lost a fortune, and the inventor foundered in a quest to create artificial rubber out of goldenrod.

But even as his inventive powers waned, Edison continued to shape the way inventing was done in America. Just before World War I, he was asked to create the new Naval Consulting Board. Characteristically, Edison spurned theoretical scientists and filled the panel with down-to-earth inventors, engineers, and corporate heads. The consulting board became involved in the new business of handing out government contracts for military research. Thus, by the time he died in 1931, the man who had come to symbolize American individual creativity had invented its corporate opposite: the military-industrial complex. □

Light Entertainers

The famous command "Lights, camera, action!" would never have entered the language without John and Anton Kliegl, the Bavarian-born brothers whose natural genius for lighting made modern moviemaking possible.

The two men emigrated to the United States in 1888, when John was nineteen and Anton sixteen. Settling in New York, they bought out their employer and started the firm of Kliegl Brothers Universal Electric Stage Lighting Company, trailblazers in the development of theatrical and movie-lighting equipment. Their most important invention was a powerful carbon-arc lamp known as the Kliegl light, later shortened to klieg light. Its powerful glare allowed moviemakers to work at night and to create standardized stage lighting conditions in the daytime.

The major problem with klieg lights was that their blazing beams could cause conjunctivitis and other eye disorders collectively called klieg eye. Rendered painfully light sensitive, actors forced to work under the bright lamps created a Hollywood trademark as famous as the Kliegl brothers' invention: the perpetual wearing of sunglasses. □

John Kliegl *(near right)* and brother Anton, who brought the bright lights that bear their name to the movies, pose with sister Julie in the only known photograph of the brothers together.

Bra Minded

The brassiere has been around at least since the Greeks wore a bandeau style called the *mastodeton* or the *apodesmos*. But it took a flash of insight by a radical French feminist to bring the garment back into modern life.

Herminie Cadolle was born to a well-off family in 1845, but she was sensitive to the libertarian ideas of the times. One of her friends was Louise Michel, the so-called Red Virgin of Montmartre, who joined the National Guard during the 1871 Commune of Paris and fought courageously as one of the Communards against government troops sent from Versailles. Shocked by the behavior of Communards and troops alike, Cadolle left France for Argentina.

The liberated woman of action soon took note of a large market for quality lingerie in Argentina and opened a business selling French underwear. It boomed. Cadolle became a globe-trotting businesswom-

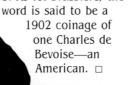

an—who found herself chafed by her stifling corset. In 1889, she returned to Paris to set up her main shop on the Rue du Chassee d'Antin and began to engineer a better undergarment. Her 1889 invention was "designed to sustain the bosom and supported by the shoulders." Called by Cadolle *le bien-être*, or "well-being," the two-piece device caused the bosom to be suspended rather than supported and let the now-separate corset shrink to accommodate the hips, leaving the upper body free. To improve her invention, she later added elastic material.

Herminie Cadolle died in 1926, but her lingerie house continues on the elegant Rue Cambon. Today's Maison Cadolle is headed by Poupie Cadolle, Herminie's great-great-granddaughter. In France, *le bien-être* has been called *le soutien-gorge* ("throat support") since 1905. As for *brassiere*, the word is said to be a 1902 coinage of one Charles de Bevoise—an American. □

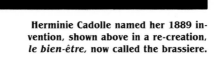

Herminie Cadolle named her 1889 invention, shown above in a re-creation, *le bien-être*, now called the brassiere.

Friese-Greene of the Movies

Almost from the moment he apprenticed to a Bristol photographer at fourteen, William Friese-Greene sensed that photography should capture the full human experience of light, shadow, color—and motion. Friese-Greene succeeded brilliantly in achieving much of this, then lost it all. Today the man who invented the motion-picture camera is remembered mainly by film historians.

He was born William Green in Bristol, England, in 1855, the son of a local craftsman. Young William had an early love for physics and chemistry, and was also an aspiring poet. He left his apprenticeship prematurely after a quarrel with his boss and opened his own successful portrait studio in the provinces, which eventually became a chain of shops in Bath, Bristol, and Plymouth. An avowed romantic, when he married Helena Friese in 1874 he added his wife's name to his own, tacking a spare *e* to Green for good measure.

Soon Friese-Greene had a good income, with hundreds of satisfied clients, enjoyed a considerable reputation as a portrait photographer, and was happy in his work. But while living in Bath, he met John Rudge, an early experimenter with a slide projector called the Biophantascope Lantern, which simulated motion by flashing a series of images on a screen. The rudimentary attempt attracted Friese-Greene completely. Struck by the possibilities of using photography to reproduce motion upon a screen, he, like so many others before and since, caught the

movie bug. Deciding to commit himself to this work, he moved to London in 1885, eventually setting up a laboratory in Holborn.

His early attempts at designing a motion-picture camera used paper film, which tore under the slightest pressure. But he had already hit upon the idea of a sprocket drive that pulled film in front of the lens while a shutter opened and closed. And he soon began to experiment with celluloid film, whose sprocket holes did not tear as readily. He incorporated celluloid film into a second camera completed in 1889. In January 1889, he first used it to photograph his cousin and young son, along with pedestrians and horse-drawn vehicles, in Hyde Park on a Sunday. When the developed images began to flicker to life on his improvised screen, Friese-Greene rushed into the street, grabbed the first person he saw—a police constable—and pulled the man into his studio to admire the results. Later that year, with a third camera, he applied to patent an "Improved Apparatus for Taking Photographs in Rapid Series." It did not work as well as his others because for some reason he had temporarily abandoned the sprocket-driven system that would eventually become standard and which he used in his fourth camera, built in 1890. And there, as he stood on the brink of a fortune, the financial side of his life collapsed.

The cost of building the prototype cameras and seeking a patent, and neglect of his lucrative studio work combined to bring him to bankruptcy and a short sentence in debtor's prison. A printing scheme for picture postcards ended in disaster. In May 1890, he sold his patent—the patent covering the basic principle of cinematography—to a merchant for £500. The new owner let the patent lapse in 1894, three years after Thomas Edison had patented his kinetoscope and the same year that the French Lumière brothers unveiled their own projector.

Friese-Greene continued to be tormented by debt and did a second term in jail for bankruptcy, but his inventive reflex continued to produce. Setting aside cinematography in favor of a fascination with x-rays, he invented a push-button device that eventually became the first x-ray examination system in Britain. He never exploited it, pursuing instead a novel ⟡

kind of inkless printing that involved the reaction of chemically sensitized paper to electricity. His idea never got off the ground. Neither did his attempts to create color film or three-dimensional images. In each of these innovative incarnations, he was able to start a company and live for a time with some stability. But nothing could arrest Friese-Greene's irresistible drift toward bankruptcy.

He had one more moment of fame in 1910, when a group of businessmen asked him to come to the United States and testify in a patent case against a film-camera monopoly. The case resulted in American recognition of Friese-Greene's 1889 patent, and his hosts paid him a thousand pounds for participating. His celebrity ended back in England, however, where he had to squeeze a living from such photographic work as he was able to find.

In 1921, the destitute sixty-six-year-old inventor attended a meeting of British film moguls in London. Alarmed by the animosity displayed among competing factions, Friese-Greene rose to speak. His face twisted by emotion, he urged cooperation but became increasingly incoherent. "I have given my life," he cried. He burst into tears, and his words lost all sense. Someone helped him back to his seat in the stunned audience. The old man sat slumped forward with his face cradled in his hands. When a friend touched him, he did not stir. "Good heavens," someone exclaimed, "I think he's dead." In his pocket they found one shilling and ten pence, Friese-Greene's total estate—and, coincidentally enough, the price of a seat at a British theater. □

Big Wheel

George Washington Gale Ferris, Jr., liked to claim he had sketched out every single detail of his most ambitious engineering project over a single dinner at a Chicago chophouse. His critics, on the other hand, sniffed that he was guilty of a trivial inventive misdemeanor: He had merely reinvented the wheel.

Born in 1859, a Nevada farmer's son, Ferris attended Rensselaer Polytechnic Institute in New York State and emerged an engineer specializing in railway tunnels and bridges, and an innovative forger of structural steel. As owner of his own company, he saw a chance to achieve fame in his profession in 1892, when the organizers of the Chicago Fair invited proposals for a centerpiece attraction. The boosters wanted one that would eclipse the wrought-iron pride of the 1889 Paris Exposition: the one-thousand-foot-high Eiffel Tower.

Ferris's true inventive talent was the scope of his imagination. He conceived of a steel wheel 250 feet in diameter, suspended between two 140-foot pyramidal towers. A total of thirty-six gondolas would be suspended from the device, each capable of carrying sixty people. The total weight of the prefabricated wheel alone was 1,200 tons, and it was powered by two 1,000-horsepower steam engines, one kept always in reserve. The cost: $350,000, about $4.5 million in 1990 currency. Transforming the conception to a structure that would stand fell to Ferris's partner, engineer William F. Gronau.

The fair backers endorsed the idea, but there was barely time to get the wheel built, and no time to test it before the monster apparatus was assembled on its site near Lake Michigan. As the casting proceeded, skeptics dubbed the project "G. W.'s cockeyed dream." But on June 21, 1893, not quite two months after the fair opened, the enormous structure began to turn—and crowds thronged. By the fair's end, one and a half million people had paid fifty cents each for a ride that took them through two revolutions in twenty minutes.

The wheel was both Ferris's triumph and his downfall. He was accused of copying it from countless sources. He and fair organizers squabbled over profits from the ride, and his fortunes plummeted. Meantime, William Sullivan of Illinois designed a portable Ferris wheel that could be put to better commercial use. Little more than four years after he had conceived of the mammoth mobile, the thirty-seven-year-old Ferris died, nearly bankrupt, in a Pittsburgh hospital. His great wheel was dismantled in 1904 and reassembled in St. Louis, Missouri, for the Louisiana Purchase Exposition.

In 1906, heeding a public outcry against the metal eyesore, wreckers detonated a hundred pounds of dynamite that knocked the wheel to the ground. According to the *Chicago Tribune's* epitaph, it slowly rotated "and then after tottering a moment like a huge giant in distress, it collapsed, slowly. . . . Within a few minutes it was a tangled mass of steel and iron forty feet high." A second hundred-pound charge finished the job. Ferris's grand invention had vanished, leaving only the echo of the inventor's name, which still graces such wheel rides today. □

Seeking to eclipse the Eiffel Tower for the 1892 Chicago Fair, George Ferris *(right)* built an enormous riding wheel that brought him fame—and financial ruin. Dismantled after the fair, the wheel was rebuilt *(below)* for the 1904 St. Louis Louisiana Purchase Exposition.

Out of Steam

Steam engines revolutionized the mechanical world, but they were relatively inefficient and not very versatile. Rudolf Diesel, a shy young German, imagined a device that was much more compact and powerful, based not on the expansion of water vapor but on that of rapidly heated air.

The middle child of Bavarians living in Paris, Diesel was born in 1858. Initially, he showed talent as an artist, but he became an engineer instead and studied thermodynamics in Augsburg. His studies convinced him that compressing air in a piston would create enough heat to ignite fuel without an electrical ignition system and that a new kind of engine could be designed to withstand the enormous pressures involved. Diesel began tinkering while he was working at a factory that made refrigeration machines. One of his early experimental models exploded, almost killing him.

In 1892, he applied for an initial patent on his compressed-air design and won partial backing from the powerful Krupp steel concern. For five years, he experimented with technology and fuels, trying everything from ammonia to peanut oil in his contraption. Eventually, he hit on the semirefined petroleum now known as diesel fuel.

From the beginning, his massive engines were a tremendous success. Because of the high temperatures and pressures within the engines, however, his invention was used only in large machines. Although popular, the engines came into common use gradually, eventually being used to power ships, locomotives, and submarines.

Diesel himself made millions from licensing fees but spent huge amounts on a grandiose mansion in Munich and numerous investments that soured in the nervous economic climate of the day. His financial troubles were matched by failing health. He suffered from gout, severe headaches, and depressions, which deepened as the pacifist-minded inventor saw Europe spiral toward war. In September 1913, less than a year before World War I erupted, Diesel prepared to make a journey to England. He went to some pains to spend time with his family and, just before leaving his wife, Martha, gave her a fine new leather bag, not to be opened, he insisted, until the following week.

On September 29, Diesel boarded the channel steamer *Dresden* in Antwerp. He did not appear the next morning at breakfast, and an officer later found Diesel's hat and his coat, neatly folded, on the stern. Twelve days later, a Belgian police boat found a body whose clothing contained a coin purse, a medicine kit, and a spectacle case, all identified as Diesel's.

But his family had seen his plan days earlier. When Martha Diesel opened the bag her vanished husband had given her, she found twenty thousand marks in cash— all that remained of the great Diesel fortune. □

Self-Starters

Charles Kettering was a shrewd, intuitive country boy who added electricity to business machines and automobiles, Freon to refrigerators, and the modern concept of the research team to American industry. Yet the man fondly called Boss Ket by his colleagues always referred to himself as a "pliers and screwdriver man." Such modesty helped make him the country's best beloved inventor, next to Thomas Alva Edison.

Born to an Ohio farming family in 1876, Kettering began studying engineering in college but dropped out because of chronic eye problems. He became a schoolteacher, then returned to college to become an electrical engineer. Practical problems intrigued him. He found a job at the National Cash Register Company, where he joined the team that invented the electrically operated cash register.

By 1909, he had moved on to found the Dayton Engineering Laboratories Company (later known as Delco), a kind of prototype for the research-and-design teams found in today's auto industry. Working with talented people drawn from his NCR group, Kettering began searching for a solution to one of the basic problems of the automobile: how to combine an ignition system, lighting, and a self-starter in a single electrical system.

At the time, cars were started with a metal crank, but it was work for the strong; most women found it difficult and dangerous to operate such vehicles. Indeed, the starter crank itself was a menace to all who used it. Often the engine's compression would snap the crank back with enough force to

break an arm. Henry Leland, the president of the Cadillac Company and a supporter of Kettering's research, had lost a friend when a balky engine had sent the crank flying into the victim's jaw, causing fatal injuries.

Kettering's revolutionary starter design worked well on a Cadillac engine set up in his shop but was too large for production models of the car. Compelled by Leland's schedule to redesign and install the starter in just one week, Kettering and his team began a blistering, round-the-clock crash program. On the advice of a mechanic who had been a steamship repairman, the teetotaling Kettering brought in plenty of rum and coffee as fuel for the frantic work ahead. The team finished on time, and the first self-starters went into the 1912 Cadillac. Eventually, they were adopted by other manufacturers as well, and many would hail Charles Kettering as an emancipator whose self-starter had put women behind the wheel of the car.

Kettering soon became the first head of General Motor's research laboratories and, eventually, a leading GM stockholder. Other inventions poured from his creative mind: the high-compression engine, four-wheel brakes, Freon refrigerants, and antiknock additives for gasoline. Kettering also experimented with radio-controlled "aerial torpedoes," forerunners of the German "buzz bombs" of World War II, and he hoped to harness the process by which plants draw energy from the sun.

With General Motors president Alfred P. Sloan, Kettering set up the Sloan-Kettering Institute for Cancer Research in New York in 1945, the year after his sister Emma succumbed to a neck tumor. When he died in 1958, the bulk of his fortune went to support philanthropy.

Throughout, Boss Ket had sustained a crusty, conservative outlook, reasoning that the modern age required an old-fashioned kind of inventor, an engineer of all work not someone trained in a narrow field. "If Thomas A. Edison, the Wright brothers, and Henry Ford had taken I.Q. tests," he told an audience near the end of his life, "they wouldn't have gotten in the bleachers." He was no snob about the craft of innovation. "To make an inventor," he once observed, "all you have to do is take his mind off the idea that it's a disgrace to fail." □

This fleet of 1912 Cadillacs was fitted with the first electrical self-starter, invented by Charles Kettering, shown above cutting his seventieth birthday cake in 1946.

Masked Man

Born in Kentucky in 1875, Garrett Morgan was the son of a freed slave. He left school in the fifth grade and migrated to Cleveland, where he eventually opened a prosperous tailoring business. His first invention was serendipitous: While trying to devise a metal polish for sewing needles, he discovered a hair straightener, starting a line of products his company sold for decades. And in 1923, he devised a three-way traffic signal that was widely used until the advent of electric traffic lights. But the major creation of his inventive career came in 1912, when his tinkering with chemicals led him to design what he called a safety hood. Intended to protect rescue workers from smoke and fumes, the device consisted of a bulky helmet with two tubes that connected to an air bag at the wearer's

back. Easy to put on and remove, the contraption could keep a man breathing for up to twenty minutes. Morgan was awarded a patent in 1914 for a "Breathing Device" and formed a company to make and sell the inhalers.

Morgan's lifesaver got its most dramatic test in 1916. An explosion at a Cleveland Waterworks tunnel trapped workers 250 feet under Lake Erie, in an atmosphere filled with dangerous fumes. Morgan used his inhaler to save thirty-two people. At first, the ensuing publicity did wonders for his National Safety Device Company, which sold safety hoods to firefighters and others forced to work in a chemically hazardous setting.

In the American south, however, Morgan was often forced to hire a white man to demonstrate his gas mask. When he himself displayed it, he adopted the identity of "Big Chief Mason, a full-blooded Indian from the Walpole Reservation in Canada." Quite simply, many white people refused to wear anything invented or produced by a black man. Indeed, when it became widely known that the Lake Erie tunnel explosion's hero was black, sales of the safety hood plummeted. □

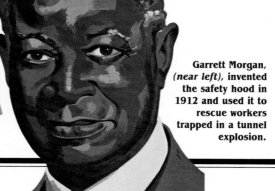

Garrett Morgan, (*near left*), invented the safety hood in 1912 and used it to rescue workers trapped in a tunnel explosion.

The Wright Stuff

They were known along the North Carolina shore as the "loony Yankees," two brothers from Dayton, Ohio, determined to invent the first machine that would fly under its own power. Engineering geniuses, the Wright brothers succeeded where so many others had failed largely because of their mastery of the most popular machine of their day: the bicycle.

Wilbur and Orville Wright were born four years apart, Wilbur in 1867, Orville in 1871, two of five children (four boys and a girl) of a bishop in the United Brethren church. Neither Wilbur nor Orville finished high school. Both were lifelong bachelors—Wilbur once joked that they could not support "a wife and a flying machine too." In 1878, their father gave the boys a rubber-band-propelled bamboo toy that skittered and hopped briefly through the air. The youngsters were fascinated and built a number of replicas of the little flying machine.

From the beginning, Wilbur and Orville were almost inseparable. Both were deeply curious about anything mechanical and loved to tinker. When Orville bought a new automobile, he immediately took it apart to see how it worked. They started to earn their living as printers, then opened a bicycle shop in Dayton to take advantage of a boom in cycling.

Eventually, they built their own bicycles, gaining experience in making precision parts and tools, and learning the workings of a chain drive. Bicycles also introduced them to the problems of

balance, for bicyclists must learn to lean into turns and to stabilize themselves against unpredictable shifts in their center of balance—much like birds. The difference is that birds have to control their direction in three dimensions, a problem no aviation pioneer had really solved in the rudimentary gliders of the day. Careful students of nature, the boys watched soaring buzzards around their home and analyzed how the birds controlled their rise and fall by moving feathers to alter the shape of their wings. Wilbur discovered the equivalent: wing warping, in which control wires twisted a model glider's wing, causing it to have more or less lift. When twisted wings were not enough for directional control, the brothers returned to their bird-watching and learned about tail feathers, the avian equivalent of rudders.

To test their wing designs, the brothers first mounted prototypes on a bicycle, but then built a wind tunnel of such sophistication that their results have hardly been improved upon in modern facilities. They also experimented with models and prototypes and, in fall 1900, began testing their gliders on the wind-swept dunes at Kitty Hawk, North Carolina. Only when their meticulous sense of design was satisfied did they build a powered model of their aircraft, which they confidently named *Flyer*.

On December 14, 1903, Wilbur tried to get *Flyer* into the air at Kitty Hawk—and smashed into the ground. Three days later, Orville climbed aboard the fragile machine, stretching himself prone across its lower wing, his feet on the rudder pedals. The airplane took off into the breeze and flew for twelve seconds—the first instance in human history of controlled, powered flight, and the very dawn of a new air age.

In the last of three more flights, the *Flyer* managed to remain aloft for fifty-nine seconds at most. Then, as the brothers planned a fourth flight, a sudden gust of wind sent the airplane cartwheeling down the dunes, demolishing it. Patiently, they built a second airplane, then a third. In 1906, they won a patent and formed a company to exploit their discovery.

Wilbur had little time to savor their great accomplishment. In 1912, only nine years after their first flight, he died suddenly of typhoid fever. Without his inseparable brother, Orville seemed to lose the desire to carry on with their pioneering venture and sold off the Wright airplane company in 1915. But he lived until 1948, long enough to see what his few seconds aloft had started. The year the first airplane pilot died, thirty-four American airlines, operating more than a thousand propeller-driven aircraft, flew nearly eight billion passenger miles. □

Krazy Kontraptions

PROFESSOR BUTTS GETS HIS THINK-TANK WORKING AND EVOLVES THE SIMPLIFIED PENCIL-SHARPENER.
OPEN WINDOW (A) AND FLY KITE (B). STRING (C) LIFTS SMALL DOOR (D) ALLOWING MOTHS (E) TO ESCAPE AND EAT RED FLANNEL SHIRT (F). AS WEIGHT OF SHIRT BECOMES LESS, SHOE (G) STEPS ON SWITCH (H) WHICH HEATS ELECTRIC IRON (I) AND BURNS HOLE IN PANTS (J). SMOKE (K) ENTERS HOLE IN TREE (L) SMOKING OUT OPOSSUM (M) WHICH JUMPS INTO BASKET (N) PULLING ROPE (O) AND LIFTING CAGE (P), ALLOWING WOODPECKER (Q) TO CHEW WOOD FROM PENCIL (R) EXPOSING LEAD. EMERGENCY KNIFE (S) IS ALWAYS HANDY IN CASE OPOSSUM OR THE WOODPECKER GETS SICK AND CAN'T WORK.

Reuben Lucius Goldberg was a skilled engineering draftsman, a stand-up comic, a reporter, and, for decades, one of the world's greatest cartoonists. Born in San Francisco in 1883, "Rube" attended the University of California, Berkeley, as an engineering student, then, his real talent discovered, joined the *San Francisco Chronicle* in 1904. Once in the newspaper business, there was no turning back for Goldberg.

Buoyed by inherited wealth, he never was the struggling artist but instead was able to try his hand at everything. He drew humor and sports, daily panels and comic strips, then moved on to become a Pulitzer Prize-winning editorial artist. Regarded by his colleagues as a cartoonist's cartoonist, he gives his name to the profession's highest honor: The Reuben is cartoonery's equivalent of Hollywood's Oscar.

But Goldberg is most widely remembered for the bizarre inventions he attributed to one Professor Lucifer Gorgonzola Butts. Mixing grand silliness with high seriousness, these devices used balloons, leaking hot-water bottles, candle flames, pulleys, strings, levers, and various animals in elaborate schemes for accomplishing simple tasks. Goldberg's Simplified Pencil Sharpener, for example, shown above, employs a flying kite, moths, an opossum, and a woodpecker in nineteen steps.

"I am credited with any machine that looks crazy," Reuben Goldberg once complained. "People coming into my studio expect me to be hanging from the chandelier." In fact, his wildly complicated, improbably improvised machines have come into the language. By definition, a Rube Goldberg machine is an overengineered solution to a simple problem—really, no solution at all. □

More than a Pretty Face

In the 1930s and 1940s, Hedy Lamarr was hailed as the world's most beautiful woman and Hollywood's most glamorous movie star. She was also an aspiring inventor, anxious to put her creations to work to help the Allies win the war.

The Vienna-born actress's career as a weaponeer began in 1940, three years after her arrival in America as Hedy Kiesler. At a Hollywood dinner party with composer George Antheil, the twenty-six-year-old beauty confessed that she had a number of ideas for inventions that could help the war effort. A fascinated Antheil and Lamarr began an intense collaboration to put one of her designs into a patentable form.

The device would send radio commands to a torpedo in coded patterns, enabling the weapon to be guided without being jammed by enemy countermeasures. Their idea amounted to a design for a variable radio tuner, whose frequency was changed from time to time by the punched instructions in a belt resembling a player-piano roll. An identical instrument was attached to a radio transmitter. When the two were started in coordinated fashion, they changed frequency in unison. Antheil and Lamarr (under her married name, Hedy Kiesler Markey) won a patent for their creation in 1942, but there is no evidence that the military ever adopted the invention.

Lamarr never applied for another patent. Much of the expertise for the radio device presumably came from Antheil, who used arrays of player pianos in some of his highly mechanized stage productions. The glamorous Lamarr's interest in the project, and her own knowledge, may have derived from her first marriage. As a young film ingénue in Vienna, she was wedded briefly to Friedrich Mandl, the owner of Hirstenberger Patronen-Fabrick Industries and one of the world's leading munitions tycoons. □

Hedy Lamarr, at left in 1941's *Ziegfeld Girl*, paired with composer George Antheil to patent a torpedo control device.

Lindbergh's Heart

"Lucky Lindy" was idolized by millions of people after he crossed the Atlantic Ocean solo in 1927. Less well remembered are the biological exploits of Charles A. Lindbergh, a self-taught mechanical prodigy who made another kind of history in one of the strangest medical partnerships of the 1930s.

Spurred on by a brilliant but eccentric surgeon, Lindbergh created a sophisticated instrument that mimicked the actions of the human heart to preserve organic tissue. Three decades after its unveiling—lifetimes in terms of medical research—Lindbergh's "perfusion pump," designed to keep organs alive outside the body, still proved to be better than anything else of its kind.

Lindbergh's intuitive mechanical talents were noticed long before he discovered flying. As a boy, he could take apart and reassemble a shotgun before he could read. He had a long love affair with motorcycles and dropped out of the University of Wisconsin to pursue his even greater love of aircraft.

After his transatlantic flight, Lindbergh developed a deep interest in biology. His fascination with cardiac medicine did not begin until 1930, when the elder sister of his wife, Anne Morrow Lindbergh, developed rheumatic heart disease. There was no cure for the condition in those days.

Lindbergh pondered the seemingly insoluble problem. "If the circulation of blood could be maintained artificially for a few minutes," he wrote later, "why couldn't the heart be stopped and its lesions repaired by the surgeon's scalpel?" He was introduced to Dr. Alexis Carrel, a Nobel laureate surgeon working at what became Rockefeller University in Manhattan. Alexis Carrel was a specialist in organ transplantation but shared Lindbergh's interest in mysticism and extrasensory perception. Viewed by many people as eccentric, Carrel favored black surgical gowns and operating rooms done in the same color, illuminated only by a skylight.

The doctor had commissioned an engineer to build a pump to help keep specialized tissue alive outside the body. The man failed. Lindbergh—struck, as he said, by the crudeness of Carrel's equip-

FIFTEEN CENTS   June 13, 1938

TIME
The Weekly Newsmagazine

Painted for TIME by S. J. Woolf

Volume XXXI   **LINDBERGH, CARREL & PUMP**   Number 24
They are looking for the fountain of age.
(See MEDICINE)

On *Time's* June 13, 1938, cover, pilot and inventor Charles Lindbergh and surgeon Alexis Carrel display their 1935 invention: a pump that took the heart's place during surgery.

ment—asked to borrow the model. Two weeks later, he returned with his own version, a major improvement over the original. Lindbergh spent the next five years—a time punctuated by the notorious kidnap-murder of his son—perfecting an instrument that would keep various organs alive, and even allow them to develop, without the risk of infection.

The elaborate design work involved creating valves and chambers that would mimic the changing pressures of the heart—a formidable exercise in 1930s engineering. As a sideline, Lindbergh invented a flask in which, as he described it, "living tissue cells could be microscopically observed and photographed while in a circulating-fluid medium."

In 1935, the two men described their work in an article in *Science* magazine. Three years later, a book, *The Culture of Organs,* was published, in which Lindbergh contributed chapters on instrument design. Once again, he became a media hero. By that time, however, Carrel had become a recluse, more interested in elitist theories of social science than in biology. Lindbergh's work was neglected, and many of his pumps were destroyed. But in 1966, U.S. Naval Research Institute workers studying the freezing of organs found Lindbergh's results on tissue survival to be better than their own. They asked the famous flier to redesign his pump to work in the extremely cold temperatures required for organic freezing and revival known as cryogenic medicine. The result: a valuable modern research tool for studying how cancer cells grow, based on the "Lone Eagle's" glass heart. □

Painkiller

The whirlpool bath known as a Jacuzzi is the quintessential symbol of the relaxed American lifestyle. Yet it was invented not as a watery playpen for the leisure class but as a relief for a son's suffering. In about 1917, Candido Jacuzzi migrated from Italy to California to join his brothers, who had come to America some years earlier and opened a machine shop, where they designed and built aviation equipment. A fatal crash of a Jacuzzi-designed monoplane in 1921, however, led them to try other fields. In 1926, another brother, Rachele, invented a water-injection pump that became the basis of the family's fortune and made them prosperous suppliers of water-system components for industry and the expanding California swimming-pool market. But all was not right in the Jacuzzi family.

From infancy, Candido's young son Kenneth had suffered from rheumatoid arthritis, a painful and crippling disorder. While the boy received pain-moderating hydrotherapy in the 1940s, his father noticed the hospital's swirling whirlpool bath used pumps not unlike those sold by the Jacuzzis. After experimentation, he produced a therapeutic bath for home use, initially sold only

through medical supply stores.

A 1950s Hollywood health craze helped to popularize the innovation, resulting in a portable design favored by athletes and other aching people on the move. By the mid-1960s, the family had produced a model that integrated pumps, jets, and tub into a self-contained unit that became an element of luxurious bathroom design. Candido became the family patriarch and reigned until 1969, when, indicted for income-tax evasion, he returned for a time to Italy. The Jacuzzis sold off their family business in 1975 for $70 million; however, whirlpool baths may always be called Jacuzzis. □

Candido Jacuzzi (right) invented his now-famous whirlpool bath to ease the pain of a son with arthritis.

The Inventor's Art

In 1944, in the pages of the British humor magazine *Punch,* readers were introduced to Nellie, a gloriously executed cartoon locomotive serving the Branch Lines of Friars Crumbling, with stops in such improbable places as Long Suffering and St. Torpid's Creek. The creation of thirty-eight-year-old Rowland Emett, Nellie was also on her way to another unlikely stop: She would be the first of Emett's inventions to become a working machine.

Emett had shown from an early age that he possessed considerable talent as both inventor and artist. Born in London in 1906, he won his first patent at thirteen, for a pneumatic acoustic control for windup record players. By the 1930s, his landscapes had been well received but not well enough to keep him during a global economic depression. He went to work as a draftsman in an engraving studio, where he sketched imaginary cars. When he tried *Punch* in 1939 and learned he could make more than four pounds a drawing, he thought his fortune was made.

In fact, his fortune would be made as an inventor of his whimsical machines. In 1950, he was asked to re-create Nellie as a working train for the Festival of Britain, a centennial celebration of the Great Exposition of 1851. Renamed the Far Tottering and Oystercreek Line, the mechanical locomotive carried millions of visitors.

Other commissions followed swiftly. In 1952, Emett built the Astroterramare for Shell Oil, and, a year later, the Hogmuddle Rotary Niggler and Fidgeter, a sixty-foot-long contraption that toured British agricultural shows. A national exposition led to a bizarre assortment of automatic devices for the home in 1956, and, in 1960, the Honeywell-Emett Forget-Me-Not Computer, a hideously elaborate machine that did everything except compute.

International fame arrived after Emett designed the inventions of Professor Potts, the eccentric protagonist of Walt Disney's 1968 film *Chitty-Chitty-Bang-Bang.* Since then Emett has delivered, among a number of other strange devices, the Rhythmical Time Fountain and the Borg-Warner Vintage Car of the Future, the Featherstone-Kite Openwork Basketweave Mark II Gentleman's Flying Machine, and two working versions of the Pussiewillow, one displayed at the U.S. National Air and Space Museum in Washington, D.C.

All of Emett's objects have in common that they reproduce in cane, cloth, and metal the delicate lines of his drawings. Serving no purpose whatever, they are inventions for invention's sake, born mostly of the necessity to smile. □

Cartoonist Rowland Emett *(below)* designed the fanciful Borg-Warner Vintage Car of the Future, then he turned it into a full-scale, functioning machine.

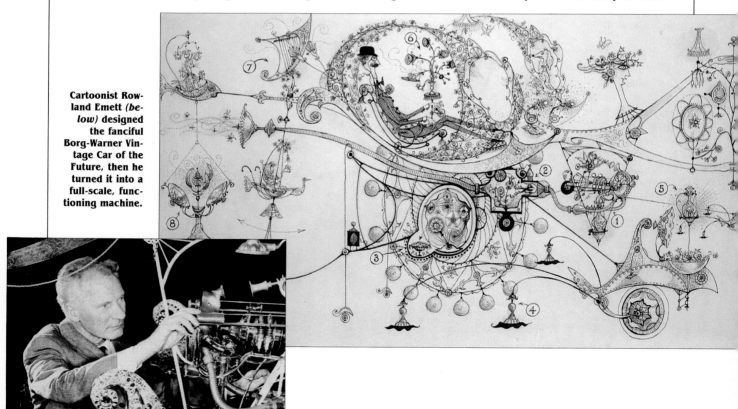

EUREKA!

The lore of invention is defined most emphatically by those explosions of sudden inspiration that occur when training, circumstance, and intuition combine to produce a brilliant creative spark—and something entirely new. These sudden insights can spring full-blown from the mysterious workshop of a singularly gifted brain or arise from the intellectual combustion that comes from the application of many good heads to a single problem. The door to discovery may also be opened by accident or coincidence.

Haphazard as such inventive leaps may seem, however, they are really creations of the subconscious inventive mind, where work proceeds around the clock, endlessly forging the ideas that, when they surface, seem to come out of nowhere, the thunderbolts and brainstorms of innovation.

Heureka!

The first recorded instant of invention took place in the public baths of the Greek city-state of Syracuse in the third century BC. As Archimedes, a mathematician and inventor already renowned for his brilliance, prepared for a reviving soak, he pondered a problem that had been presented to him by his friend and leader, King Hiero II. Hiero had given his goldsmith a quantity of gold to be fashioned into a crown. When the object was delivered, however, the king began to suspect the artisan of having secretly alloyed the pure gold with less precious silver and pocketing the excess gold. The royal challenge to Archimedes: Determine the real composition of the crown without disfiguring it in any way.

With this puzzle on his mind, Archimedes lowered his contemplative hulk into the bath, which had been filled to the brim. As he sank into the water, the tub overflowed—and Archimedes had his solution. "*Heureka!*" he shouted (I have found it!). He leaped from his bath and ran home, streaking through the streets of Syracuse with the principle of water displacement taking form in his head.

What Archimedes had deduced in the bath was that a submerged body displaces water according to the object's volume. Since gold is almost twice as dense as silver—a cubic inch holds more than eleven ounces of gold but less than six ounces of silver—an object made of gold would occupy less volume than one of the same weight made of gold and silver. Sure enough, when he submerged equal weights of silver and gold, he found that the denser gold displaced less water. By comparing the water displaced by the crown to that displaced by an equal weight of pure gold, he was able to confirm Hiero's suspicions. The crown displaced more water and therefore could not be made of pure gold. The fate of the thieving goldsmith is lost to history, but future generations received the term still used to mark such moments of discovery: *Eureka!* □

A sixteenth-century German woodcut shows Greek inventor Archimedes at his moment of watery insight.

Chip Shot

A fit of spite became an act of creation for George Crum, the head chef at Moon's Lake House resort in Saratoga Springs, New York. One day in 1853, Crum, furious after a customer complained that his French fries were "too thick and soggy" and "not salty enough," decided to seek culinary vengeance. He sliced some potatoes paper-thin, fried them to a singed crispy brown, doused them copiously with salt, and presented them with a flourish to the discontented diner.

The customer tasted one, then smiled and popped another, thereby inaugurating what would become a national habit. Before long, the Saratoga Chips, as Crum's accidental delicacy was dubbed, could be found on menus all across the country. Today the average American consumes about six pounds of Crum's revenge—potato chips—every year. □

George Crum, shown at right with his wife, invented the potato chip in 1853 at Moon's Lake House *(above)*.

Prime Mauver

William Perkin was a man of unusual—and precocious—vision. At the age of twelve, he knew that chemistry would be his lifelong passion. By the time he was eighteen, in 1856, he was assistant to the noted organic chemist August Wilhelm von Hoffmann at London's Royal College of Chemistry.

Hoffmann knew that aniline, an organic substance made of carbon, hydrogen, and nitrogen, could be distilled from coal tar, a waste by-product of coal-gas production. He had also found that another coal-tar distillate, called allyltoluidine, seemed to be similar to quinine. Obtained solely from the bark of the tropical cinchona tree, quinine was the only effective remedy for the malarial fever endemic to many regions then under British colonial rule. Hoffmann believed that it might be possible to synthesize quinine from allyltoluidine in the laboratory, and, with characteristic enthusiasm, his young assistant attacked the problem.

Working obsessively in his improvised home laboratory, Perkin labored day and night through his Easter holiday, but his attempts to manipulate the chemicals left him with only a reddish brown mud. Others might have given up, but not Perkin.

He decided to replace the allyltoluidine with a simpler compound, aniline. This time he got not ruddy but black sludge. Some instinct pushed Perkin to take one further step. He boiled the sludge into a crystalline precipitate, which, when added to water, produced a deep purplish stain. Trying the solution as a dye, he discovered that it had spectacular properties as a permanent coloring for silk. He called the crystals mauveine and their rich color mauve, after the reddish purple flowers of the common mallow plant, which the French called *mauve*. Perkin's discovery launched Britain's synthetic aniline dye industry and made coal tar a valuable industrial product. By 1874, at the age of thirty-seven, Perkin had become a rich and honored man, financially able to return to the pure chemistry that had always been his vocation. His widely used color became the symbol of the 1890s—the so-called Mauve Decade of complacent prosperity. In 1906, Perkin was knighted by Edward VII for his discovery fifty years before. □

Mauve silk became a symbol of the late-Victorian era after William Perkin (above) stumbled upon a purplish dye in coal tar.

99.44 Percent Luck

In 1878, officials at the Procter & Gamble soap and candle factory in Cincinnati, Ohio, found themselves in a quandary. Company headquarters had been deluged recently with bewildering requests for "more of the soap that floats." Although the company had just introduced a new product called White Soap, a fragrant concoction intended to compete with fine soaps from Spain, no one knew of a buoyant bar.

The mystery cleanser was finally traced to a factory accident, which occurred when a worker left for lunch without turning off the mixer in a vat of White Soap, causing the batch to incorporate more than the customary amount of air. After realizing his mistake, he had decided to send the overwhipped mixture on through the normal production process, and the airy batch was hardened, chopped into bars, and sent to market. When it hit the stores, consumers tried it and were delighted by the unsinkable soap that refused to get lost in murky water.

With crack marketing reflexes, Harley Procter, a son of the company's founder, ordered that henceforth all batches of White Soap be overmixed. Then, searching for a better name for his bobbing bonanza, Procter took inspiration from a quote from the Forty-fifth Psalm: "All thy garments smell of myrrh and aloes and cassia out of ivory palaces." To this day, the famous floating soap is still called Ivory. □

An Ivory arch of "the soap that floats" appeared in a 1908 advertisement from Procter & Gamble, where the first buoyant bars, produced accidentally in 1878, were skillfully marketed by Harley Procter (*above*).

The Shining

"Chance favors the prepared mind," the French chemist Louis Pasteur once said, and the story of one of his own colleagues—scientist Count Hilaire de Chardonnet (*right*)—illustrates dramatically the truth of his observation. During the late 1800s, Chardonnet and Pasteur worked together on stopping an epidemic among silkworms. In the course of their collaboration, Chardonnet became fascinated by the mulberry-leaf-eating insect's ingenuity in spinning its radiant thread. Surely, he thought, man could study this process and learn to produce silken threads of his own.

As Chardonnet moved on to other projects, he retained that latent wish to imitate the silkworm. One day in 1878, while coating photographic plates in a darkroom, he

accidentally broke a bottle of collodion on his worktable. Rather than clean the thick liquid up right away, he left it. By the time he got back to it, the solution was a sticky mass. As Chardonnet rubbed across the spill with his cloth, he pulled up long filaments—filaments that looked remarkably like silk threads.

Others might have seen only an ugly mess; Chardonnet saw the future. An independently wealthy man, he financed his own experiments and spent the next six years perfecting the first man-made fiber for use in textiles, and developing a way to produce it commercially. In effect, he followed his early impulse and imitated the silkworm. Like natural silk, his fiber was made from mulberry leaves and extruded through fine apertures that, like the silkworms' organs, are still called spinnerets.

"Chardonnet silk" was the hit of the Paris Exhibition of 1889. Later named rayon—for the way it gathered rays of light—the new synthetic also acquired a gruesome nickname: mother-in-law silk. Because the first rayon fabrics were highly flammable, the perfect gift for an unpopular mother-in-law was said to be a rayon dress—and a kitchen match. □

Invisible Light

On November 8, 1895, Wilhelm Röntgen, a physics professor at Würzburg University in Germany, was working late into the night in a small laboratory below his home. A quiet but intense man, the fifty-year-old Rhinelander was experimenting with a Crookes tube—a scientific device consisting of a glass cylinder from which most of the air had been exhausted to create a vacuum. Scientists had noted that when an electrical current was applied to the apparatus, a faint green glow illuminated the tube; this unexplained phenomenon was the subject of the professor's nocturnal experiment.

Curious to know whether opaque paper would block the glow, as it did regular light, Röntgen darkened his lab completely and encased the tube in an envelope of black cardboard that fit over it with "tolerable closeness," as he described it later. When he turned the tube's current on, Röntgen noticed something very strange. The cardboard seemed to block the tube's glow effectively, for the room remained completely dark; but a peculiar fluorescence shone from a bench area off to one side. When he increased the electrical current, the fluorescence brightened; when he switched off the

current, the fluorescence died.

Röntgen quickly flicked on the lights and moved to the bench. The source of the fluorescence, he discovered, was a cardboard screen coated with barium platinocyanide—a substance that glows, or fluoresces, when exposed to light. But there had been no light—that is, there had been no *visible* light.

Certain that he was on the brink of an unprecedented discovery, the tall, bearded Röntgen began working feverishly, experimenting night and day to discover as much as he could about this invisible form of light. He deduced that the rays were not beams of energetic parti-

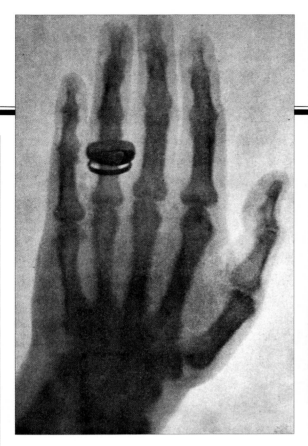

cles but the same kind of energy as light waves, except that their wavelength was ten thousand times shorter than that of visible light. He decided to call the mysterious emanations x-rays, because in science *x* is the variable that represents the unknown.

Another peculiarity of the mysterious rays was their ruinous effect on photographic plates, even those that were carefully wrapped and stored. Discovering one such ruined plate in his desk drawer, Röntgen *(above, right)* decided to develop it. To his surprise, the developed plate had the image of a key recorded on it with perfect clarity. Determined to find a scientific answer to this puzzle, Röntgen searched until he found the matching real key—lying on top of the desk, between the x-ray source and the stored plate.

Noting that in such x-ray images substances more impervious to the rays were recorded as darker shad-

ows, he began exposing different materials to x-rays. The denser the material, he discovered, the less transparent it was to the passage of x-rays. One day, to confirm a discovery that a thin layer of lead was almost completely opaque to the all-seeing radiation, Röntgen held a lead disk in front of the Crookes tube. As expected, he saw the shadow of the disk on the fluorescent screen and more: the chilling image of his own thumb and finger bones as dark, legible members inside the barely visible shadow of his flesh.

Six weeks after his night of discovery, Röntgen presented his findings to the world. A widely circulated x-ray photograph at the time was the skeletal image of Röntgen's wife's hand, the lump of her wedding ring clearly visible around one finger bone *(above, left)*. Many, including Bertha Röntgen herself, shivered at such skeletal images, believing them to be

omens of impending death. Others worried that x-ray photographs would make privacy an extinct commodity; one British manufacturer advertised x-ray-proof underwear as a must for the modest.

But scientists quickly put Röntgen's rays to work. Just twenty days after the Röntgen presentation, x-rays were used in Germany to examine a finger injured by a bullet. Within two months, x-ray photographs helped New Hampshire physicians treat a bone fracture. Soon scientists and doctors everywhere were perfecting new uses for the invisible light.

A modest and reserved man, Röntgen refused most honors except the first Nobel Prize awarded in physics, which he received in 1901. He continued quietly with his work until the age of seventy-eight, when he died of intestinal cancer—induced, some believe, by decades of exposure to the rays that made his name immortal. □

Rough Stuff

In 1879, the brothers E. Irvin and Clarence W. Scott launched a paper-products business in Philadelphia and, early in the new century, began marketing what was then still a novelty: toilet paper. Called Waldorf Tissue, it sold in small, discreet rolls that bore the slogan "soft as old linen."

One day in 1907, a large order of the by-then famous ScotTissue arrived from the paper mill and was deemed defective. The paper in the huge parent rolls—long tubes that were cut down to household size at the Scott factory—was excessively heavy and wrinkled and nothing like old linen. It presented the Scotts with a railroad car full of paper too tough to sell.

The flawed shipment was scheduled for return, but Irvin Scott's son Arthur had another idea. Why not cut the heavy paper into rolls perforated to provide towel-size sheets? Arthur's idea was put into action, and the first paper towels went to market, first as Sani-

A bad batch of paper inspired the invention of Scot-Towels, a bonanza for the company headed by Scott brothers E. Irvin (near right) and Clarence W.

Towels, sold primarily for use in public buildings. As their price dropped, the paper towels became more acceptable as a substitute for cloth kitchen towels in the home.

By 1931, Arthur Scott's improvised response to a shipping error had resulted in the ubiquitous ScotTowels, selling for twenty-five cents a roll. □

Moldy Medicine

In 1928, Alexander Fleming, a Scottish bacteriologist, was working at St. Mary's Hospital in London. Since the First World War, his research had been guided largely by his experiences in the British Army Medical Corps, where he had been forced to watch helplessly as gangrene and septicemia took their deadly toll. At St. Mary's, Fleming had been growing research cultures of the staphylococcus bacteria, which can send infection

raging through a hospital ward.

Returning from a short vacation, Fleming discovered that some of his culture dishes had become exposed to the atmosphere and were now contaminated by mold. He tossed the ruined experiments in the trash. Just then a lab assistant passed by, and Fleming, wishing to share his frustration, retrieved the dishes. With this fortuitous second look at a phenomenon he had dismissed, Fleming noticed some-

thing curious. In the areas invaded by mold, the bacteria had receded. Perhaps, he thought, this fungus was the very thing he had been looking for—a kind of magic bullet against infection.

When Fleming began testing molds of all kinds—he even scraped specimens from friends' shoes—he discovered just how fortunate his accidental discovery had been. Of the thousands of molds that might have contaminated his dish, it had been one called *Penicillium*, a genus com-

The three Nobel laureate discoverers of penicillin: from left, Howard Florey, Ernst Chain, and Alexander Fleming.

prising some 650 strains, only a few of which can effectively fight bacteria. The spore that had drifted into his inadvertently unsealed cultures had happened to be one of these. But here his luck ran out: Fleming was unable to isolate and stabilize the substance he called penicillin. Tantalizing as it was, his discovery was temporarily ignored.

Nearly a decade later, with Europe poised on the edge of another great war, an Oxford University team headed by Australian pathologist Howard Florey and German-born biochemist Ernst Chain had resumed work on identifying natural substances that attack bacteria. Some samples of Fleming's original culture were in a lab nearby, and when the team—which now had the technical knowledge to isolate penicillin from the mold—began experimenting with it, they obtained dramatic results. When a crude powder, which later proved to be less than 2 percent penicillin, was diluted a million times, it cured mice that had been deliberately infected with bacteria.

The onset of World War II created a great need for an infection-fighting medicine. Aware of the importance of their work, team members rubbed spores of the precious mold inside their pockets to help ensure its survival during the aerial assault against London. But growing penicillin mold was a slow process. After eight months of cultivating it in everything from baking tins to bedpans, the researchers had just enough pure powder to try treating one human. It was administered to a policeman suffering from acute blood poisoning, and for five days, he showed a remarkable recovery. Then the powder ran out, and he died.

When the war prevented British chemical firms from helping with mass production of penicillin, the United States came to the rescue. In a pharmaceutical laboratory in Peoria, Illinois, chance once again made the difference between success and failure. An assistant nicknamed Moldy Mary—she had the daily task of gathering moldy produce from local markets—brought in a melon covered with mold. Researchers in the Peoria lab had been looking for a more prolific strain of mold, and the latest melon had it. By 1943, the new miracle drug was saving the lives and limbs of many wounded soldiers.

In 1945, Fleming, Florey, and Chain shared the Nobel Prize in physiology and medicine for their development of penicillin and for opening the way to the antibiotic drugs that would revolutionize the treatment of bacterial disease. □

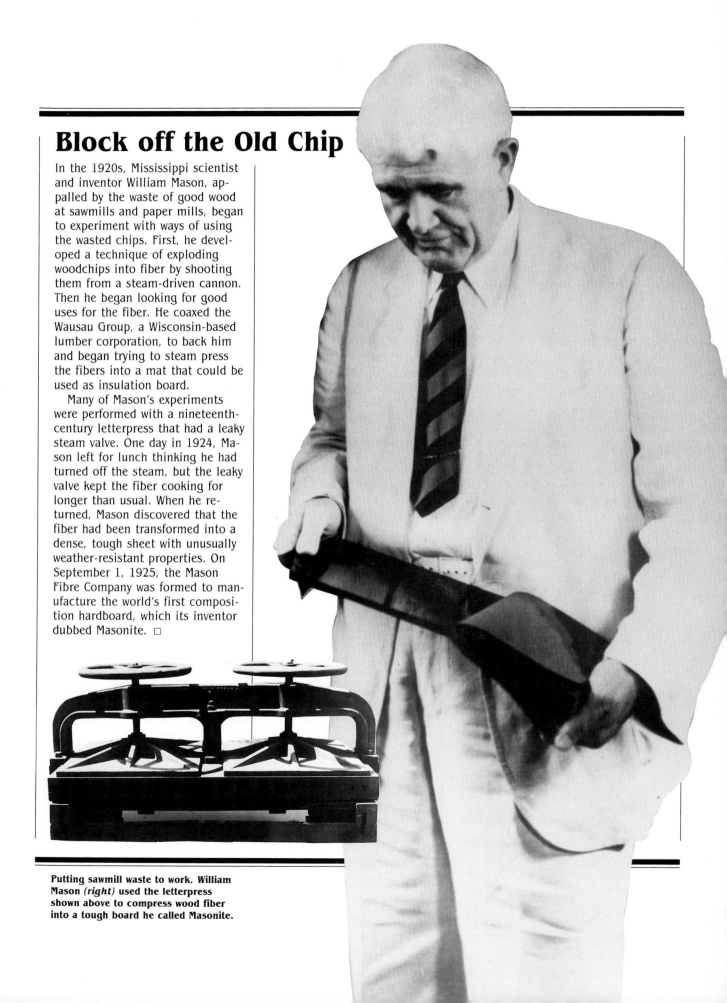

Block off the Old Chip

In the 1920s, Mississippi scientist and inventor William Mason, appalled by the waste of good wood at sawmills and paper mills, began to experiment with ways of using the wasted chips. First, he developed a technique of exploding woodchips into fiber by shooting them from a steam-driven cannon. Then he began looking for good uses for the fiber. He coaxed the Wausau Group, a Wisconsin-based lumber corporation, to back him and began trying to steam press the fibers into a mat that could be used as insulation board.

Many of Mason's experiments were performed with a nineteenth-century letterpress that had a leaky steam valve. One day in 1924, Mason left for lunch thinking he had turned off the steam, but the leaky valve kept the fiber cooking for longer than usual. When he returned, Mason discovered that the fiber had been transformed into a dense, tough sheet with unusually weather-resistant properties. On September 1, 1925, the Mason Fibre Company was formed to manufacture the world's first composition hardboard, which its inventor dubbed Masonite. □

Putting sawmill waste to work, William Mason (right) used the letterpress shown above to compress wood fiber into a tough board he called Masonite.

The Untouchable

One morning in 1938, Roy Plunkett, a young chemist just two years out of Ohio State University, stood in his lab in a state of confusion. As a researcher for the Du Pont Company, Plunkett had been experimenting with different gases, trying to develop a new, nontoxic, nonflammable refrigerator coolant. The day before, Plunkett and his assistant, Jack Rebok, had filled a cylinder with an obscure gas—tetrafluoroethylene—and stored it on Dry Ice. Now, Rebok was insisting, the cylinder was empty.

Others might have shrugged and chalked it up to just another routine laboratory mishap. But Plunkett's curiosity was piqued. He weighed the cylinder and found that it could not be empty. Then he cut it open and discovered that it was lined with a greasy white powder. Realizing instantly that the gas had polymerized into a peculiar solid, he began subjecting the powder to a series of tests. The powder proved to be virtually inert. It was resistant to temperatures from 400 degrees below zero to 500 above and resistant to virtually all solvents and acids. It also had the lowest friction coefficient of any known solid—in other words, it was very slippery.

Although Du Pont knew it had an unusual product, the stickless material was expensive to make and no one knew quite what to do with it. Then, during World War II, the Manhattan Project—America's effort to build an atomic bomb—created an urgent need for gaskets and linings that could resist the corrosive uranium hexafluoride used in producing the fissionable uranium 235 for the first bomb. Plunkett's discovery was drafted for the task—and classified as secret information until 1946.

But not until 1956, when nonstick pans lined with a material called Teflon went on sale, did the public become familiar with the substance. Although still associated with cookware, that application accounts for less than 5 percent of Teflon's present uses. Today the amazingly versatile material is used in everything from rain gear and artificial aortas to spacesuits and space-faring insulation. In fact, when astronauts returning to the moon examined equipment left by earlier expeditions, they found that much of the gear had deteriorated badly under the harsh ultraviolet radiation of the sun—except wiring insulated with Teflon. □

Radio Range

In 1946, fifty-two-year-old Percy L. Spencer was in his laboratory at the Raytheon Manufacturing Company, in Lexington, Massachusetts, conducting experiments with a magnetron, a new kind of vacuum tube that produced an extremely shortwave form of radio energy called microwaves. The device had been invented at England's Birmingham University in 1940 as part of the British wartime development of radar but had not been widely applied since.

Spencer was in some respects an unlikely candidate for such work. Born to a poor family in Maine, he was taken in by an aunt as an infant after his father was killed in a mill accident and his mother abandoned him. With little formal education, he had come up in the world largely by virtue of his strong, innate grasp of how things work. By 1925, he had become a factory supervisor at Raytheon, a company that based most of its business on a vacuum tube. When he intuitively solved a difficult tube-design problem, the company moved him to the laboratory, where, some twenty years later, he began work on the magnetron.

Reaching a pause in the day's experiment, Spencer stuck a hand into his pocket to retrieve a candy bar—and noticed something curious. The chocolate was a gooey mess, although he had felt no appreciable heat. Something had melted it. Immediately, the intuitive Spencer wondered whether the chocolate had somehow been melted by radio waves emitted from the magnetron.

To test his intuition, Spencer scattered some corn kernels near the device and switched on the magnetron. Soon there was popcorn all over the lab. He placed an egg in a wastebasket and set it in front of the magnetron. When the egg exploded, Spencer leaped straight to the scientific crux of ◊

the mess: The magnetron's waves had heated the egg from the inside out, causing pressure to build and the egg to explode.

In fact, Spencer was exactly right. The magnetron's short microwaves were of just the right length to agitate water molecules in the foods, thereby creating an interior heat that cooked from the inside out. For the first time, something had been cooked without the application—direct or indirect—of fire.

Raytheon soon launched a contest among its employees to name the new "radio ovens" that the company planned to market and settled on Radarange. The first of these ovens was a refrigerator-size monster chockablock with tubes, wires, fans, and a tiny cooking space. It was installed in Thompson's Spa restaurant in Boston that very year. In 1989, more than ten and a half million microwave ovens were sold worldwide, all derived from Spencer's moment of accident and intuition not quite half a century earlier. □

Odd Blob

Assigned to experiment with possible synthetic substitutes for rubber during World War II, General Electric engineer James Wright mixed some boric acid and silicone oil in a test tube and let the substances react. As he had hoped, the combination of materials created a rubbery blob. It was not synthetic rubber, however, but a material with properties all its own.

When Wright dropped a piece of the blob on the floor, it bounced right back. It snapped when jerked, but stretched when gently pulled. It shattered if struck, but slowly oozed into a puddle if left alone. G.E. engineers were fascinated by the contradictory properties of the material, which they dubbed Nutty Putty. Samples were sent out from the New Haven, Connecticut, lab where Wright had discovered it to specialists around the world in the hope that someone would think of a practical use for the bouncing blobs. No one did, however, and the peculiar substance remained a kind of inside joke among the engineers at New Haven.

Six years later, in 1949, toystore owner Ruth Fallgatter encountered the taffylike stuff at a New Haven cocktail party and was impressed. After consulting with her marketing adviser, Peter Hodgson—who acquired rights to Nutty Putty from General Electric—Fallgatter decided to feature Nutty Putty in her store's catalog. Offered in a clear plastic case for two dollars, the putty outsold every item in the catalog except Crayola crayons.

Sensing great potential, Hodgson asked Fallgatter to become his partner in putty pushing. When she declined, he decided to go it alone, borrowing $147 to buy the inaugural batch of what he decided to call Silly Putty. Packaged in egg-shaped containers, the putty went on sale in Neiman-Marcus and Doubleday Book shops in New York in 1950. By August, with a boost from a write-up in the "Talk of the Town" section of the *New Yorker* magazine, Silly Putty had become an overnight sensation. Wright's concoction eventually made Hodgson a multimillionaire.

Since 1950, more than 200 million eggs of the "toy with one moving part" have been sold, mostly to children. But the putty has also filled other, more adult needs. On the *Apollo 8* mission to the moon, for instance, astronauts used Silly Putty to anchor floating objects. Athletes and arthritis patients squeeze it to improve their grip, and would-be nonsmokers manipulate it as a calming hedge against nicotine fits. □

Springtime

During a ship's sea trials in 1943, twenty-five-year-old engineer Richard James was experimenting with coil springs as a way of isolating delicate navigational instruments from the vibrations of the ship. One of the springs rolled off a table and hit the deck, where it bounced back and forth until the energy of its fall had dissipated. Intrigued, James saw in that bouncing motion the seed of an idea and, once back ashore in Philadelphia, set about finding the right coil for the device that the spring had inspired.

In 1945, after James had borrowed $500 and spent every spare moment perfecting his invention, he had the spring he wanted: a long metal coil that could walk down inclines end over end, its coils rippling like something alive. Flipping through a dictionary, his wife, Betty, came up with what she thought would make a great name for the toy: Slinky.

The Jameses finally debuted their new device in 1945 on a rainy November night at Gimbels in Philadelphia. Passersby seemed mesmerized by the walking springs, and within ninety minutes, the entire stock of 400 Slinkies had sold out at a dollar apiece. After a similar demonstration a few years later in New York's Macy's, the store had to stop carrying the toy temporarily because the crowds it drew created a fire hazard.

Today James Industries Inc., in Hollidaysburg, Pennsylvania, goes through some 100,000 tons of steel a year to keep the world happily supplied with the sixty-five-foot lengths of coiled wire that have been a favorite toy for almost half a century. Although part of its charm is its seeming simplicity, a Slinky in motion actually demonstrates some rather profound laws of physics, including the law of inertia (by tending to continue moving once set in motion) and Hooke's law (by returning to its original shape after being stretched). In 1980, the Franklin Institute Science Museum in Philadelphia put on a Slink-a-thon to honor the toy and its physics.

Indeed, while children remain the primary Slinky fans, the walking springs have also been put to more innovative use—as a makeshift radio antenna in Vietnam, for instance, and as part of a pecan-picking machine in Georgia. Slinkies have even made guest appearances at an international exhibit in Moscow and aboard NASA's space shuttle in 1985, where one demonstrated the effects of zero gravity on springs. □

Dance of the Atoms

The popular view of chemical research may be one of endless experimentation in test-tube-lined laboratories, but some advances in chemistry have sprung from a more mysterious source within the chemist's mind. Such was the case with German chemist Friedrich August Kekulé von Stradonitz, who in 1865 had a vivid daydream that revealed to him the chemical structure of benzene—the hexagonal ring of six carbon and six hydrogen atoms that underlies much of modern organic chemistry.

"The atoms were gamboling before my eyes," Kekulé would later describe his vision. "I saw how, frequently, two smaller atoms united to form a pair; how a larger one embraced two smaller ones . . . whilst the whole kept whirling in a giddy dance." As the dream continued, Kekulé began to see long chains of atoms, "all twining and twisting in snake-like motion. But look! What was that? One of the snakes had seized hold of his own tail, and the form whirled mockingly before my eyes."

Curiously, the vision of a snake swallowing its tail was a familiar ancient symbol, referred to as Ouroboros by students of alchemy, the earliest form of chemistry. But Kekulé was able to translate his serpentine vision into one of the actual building blocks of chemistry, the benzene ring. □

A dream guided Friedrich August Kekulé von Stradonitz (*below*) to a hexagon of carbon and hydrogen atoms called the benzene ring.

Tally Ho!

James Ritty was on vacation in 1878 when he was struck with a brilliant solution for a problem at home. As a restaurant owner in Dayton, Ohio, Ritty had been frustrated time and again by sticky-fingered employees who stole from his business. In the hustle and bustle of the working day, it was difficult to keep track of sales and impossible to know what an honest tally at the end of each day might be. Away from it all, on a ship bound for Europe, Ritty suddenly found his answer.

He was taking a tour of the vessel's facilities when he came across the cyclometer, a machine that automatically counted each turn made by the ship's propeller. Watching the device at work, Ritty mused on inventing a counting machine of his own, one that would add up the sales his restaurant made each day. When he returned to Dayton, he acted on his idea and, in 1879, invented the cash register.

Ritty's early prototype looked more like a clock than the familiar registers seen in stores and restaurants today, but it performed the same basic functions. When an employee pressed down the amount of a sale, two hands on the face of Ritty's machine would swing to the appropriate numbers; at the same time, the machine kept a running tally of total sales by adding successive entries. Later models added a cashdrawer and then a bell, to let owners know when the drawer was open. □

Tired of his employees' pilfering, James Ritty (above) invented the first cash register, a clocklike device similar to the one shown at right.

Light-handed

In 1890, Conrad Hubert left his Russian homeland to escape the persecution of Jews and sailed to America. It was a time of upheaval and hardship for Hubert, who had owned his own distillery in Russia but now faced an uncertain future in a land he did not know.

Working at a variety of menial jobs, the thirty-five-year-old immigrant found himself always struggling to survive. Still, he dreamed and schemed, searching for a strategy to strike it rich. One day in 1898, Hubert's friend Joshua Lionel Cowen showed him an electric flowerpot he had invented. When a button was pressed, a small, battery-powered electric bulb illuminated the flowers.

In that tiny flash of light, Hubert saw his salvation. He bought the idea from Cowen for almost nothing and redesigned the device, placing the battery and bulb inside a tube and calling it an "electric hand torch." Thus the flashlight was born. Hubert founded the American Ever-Ready Company to market his new invention, and by the time he died in 1928, his estate was valued at about eight million dollars. Hubert's friend Cowen never regretted selling his flowerpot idea, however, for his interests had shifted to the invention for which he himself became famous: the Lionel electric model train. □

Later models of Conrad Hubert's "electric hand torch," such as the 1911 model shown at right with its battery, were dubbed flashlights by *Field and Stream* magazine and were produced by the inventor's American Ever-Ready Company.

Oar No More

On a sultry August day in 1906, twenty-nine-year-old Ole Evinrude was on a lakeside picnic with his girlfriend, Bess Emily Cary. Bess expressed a wish for cooling ice cream, and Ole set out to find her some. It meant rowing two miles across Wisconsin's Lake Okauchee to get Bess her sweet, and by the time he returned, the ice cream was cold soup.

But if the arduous mission had produced melted ice cream, it had also given Evinrude serious food for thought. If there had been a motor on that boat, he mused, his gallant gesture would not have been for naught.

Few men of his day were better qualified to put his idea to a test. Since the age of ten, when he had quit school to help his father on their family farm, the young Norwegian immigrant had been cultivating what seemed to be an innate mechanical genius. By 1906, he had run machine shops and plants where auto engines were designed and built.

Moreover, Evinrude seemed to possess a latter-day Viking's intuitive feel for boats. As a boy of fifteen, he had enraged his land-loving father—who had lost three uncles to the sea—by secretly building himself a sailboat. When his father chopped the vessel to pieces, the undaunted Evinrude secretly built himself another. Although Evinrude had never sailed in his life and had constructed the craft without any formal plans, both builder and boat proved eminently seaworthy.

These two strands of talent came together in Evinrude's invention. He appeared from his workshop

Inspired by the ice cream craving of his sweetheart, Bess *(inset)*, and a futile four-mile row, Ole Evinrude *(above)* invented the outboard motor.

one day in 1909 and showed Bess—now his wife—the outboard boat motor he had finally built. Bess compared the contraption to a coffee grinder at first, but when Ole returned bursting with enthusiasm after a test run on the Kinnickinnic River, she saw the motor's great potential.

She urged her husband to refine his design, and in 1909, the first ten Evinrude outboards, weighing in at sixty-two pounds and mustering one and a half horsepower each, went to market, selling for sixty-two dollars apiece. Bess, discovering a muse of her own, wrote an advertisement that read: "Don't row! Throw the oars away! Use an Evinrude motor." The response was tremendous, and a new American industry and pastime—motorboating—was launched.

Then, realizing that the winter months might be devastatingly slow for their fledgling company, Bess wrote to several foreign companies in an effort to stir up sales abroad. In one of those happy accidents that mark the progress of invention, a young Danish clerk named Oluf Mikkelsen was emptying the trash in one of these firms when a crumpled letter with the familiar Scandinavian name Evinrude at its top caught his eye. After reading Bess's letter, Mikkelsen persuaded his boss to import the Evinrude motor to Norway, Sweden, and Denmark, thus stimulating the Evinrudes' idle winter production line. Ole Evinrude, the boy with Viking blood, had come full circle.

In 1913, worried about Bess's health and ready for a rest, Ole decided to retire. He sold his business and set out with his wife and son, Ralph, on an extended tour of the country, first by automobile and then in a custom-built cabin cruiser. But by 1919, after a six-year hiatus, he was back at the drawing board, and in 1921 Ole Evinrude introduced a new lightweight aluminum motor—the Evinrude Light Twin Outboard, called ELTO for short. In 1929, he became president of the conglomerate Outboard Motors Corporation, where he remained until 1934, when, just fourteen months after the loss of the wife who had inspired him, he died. □

On the Level

From the age of six, when he presented his aunt with his first invention—a special horseradish grater—Elmer Ambrose Sperry seemed obsessed with anything new and better. His entire life was punctuated with moments of sudden, inspired inventive flashes in which a new idea seemed almost to hang in the air before his eyes, waiting for him to see it.

As a teenager, he had pored eagerly over every issue of the Patent Office's *Official Gazette.* By 1876, when he was sixteen, Sperry's special brand of brainpower had become so evident that the YMCA in his hometown of Cortland, New York, helped send him to the Centennial Exposition in Philadelphia. Only a few years later, in 1880, Sperry founded Sperry Electric Company, the first of several companies he would establish over the course of his life to exploit the more than 350 inventions that he patented. Sperry Electric Company had a great deal of success installing arc light systems designed by the young inventor, but before long Sperry's restless mind turned to new fields, and he was designing innovative mining equipment, streetcars, and electric automobiles.

In 1907, Sperry's attention was drawn by the gyroscope—a familiar child's toy consisting of a wheel mounted within other wheels in such a way that it can turn freely and seek its own orientation in space. As long as the toy gyro continued spinning, it righted itself continuously. Surely, Sperry thought, the world could make some more productive use of this remarkable principle. In fact, in 1852, a French scientist named Foucault had used the gyroscope to demonstrate the rotation of the

Capturing his sudden inspirations in sketches like the ones at left, Elmer Sperry (*above*) put gyroscopes to work in automatic pilots.

earth, and in the early 1900s, a German named Hermann Anschütz-Kaempfe had developed a basic gyrocompass as a more reliable alternative to the magnetic compass. But Sperry felt that the gyroscope was the key to something more and waited for his special muse to pounce.

Inspiration, when it arrived, came suddenly. While sleeping on a Europe-bound ship, Sperry was thrown from his berth during a storm. Immediately he realized what he could do with the balancing properties of a gyroscope. In 1910, he formed the Sperry Gyroscope Company, which, in the years that followed, introduced a whole series of gyroscope-based inventions. He devised a highly accurate gyrocompass and gyrostabilizers used to counter the rolling motions of ships and airplanes. From these, Sperry proceeded to develop several automatic-pilot devices, including his famous Metal Mike, an automatic steering device for ships that in 1928 was heralded as having piloted a steam tanker on its course from San Francisco to Auckland, New Zealand, for twenty-one straight days. "There were cobwebs on her steering wheel when the Auckland pilot climbed aboard," a story in *Popular Science* reported.

To the end of his life, Sperry retained his characteristic ability to be inspired by almost anything. On a hot day in June 1930, as he lay dying in a hospital room, he watched attentively as a block of ice was placed in front of a fan to cool him. "Put it in a large pan and fill the pan with water," said the man who had always looked for a better way. "That will increase . . . the effectiveness." □

A Sudden Chill

From the start, Clarence Birdseye seemed to have a penchant for plants and animals. Born in Brooklyn, New York, in 1886, as a boy he ran an advertisement offering instructions in the art of taxidermy. As a student at Amherst College, he worked on the side collecting frogs for the Bronx Zoo and rats for a biology professor at Columbia University. When he found himself still short of funds, he left school and headed west as a field naturalist for the U.S. Biological Survey.

Out in the land of coyote and bobcat, Birdseye had his first experience with fur trading, a business interest that, in 1912, took him to the distant Canadian peninsula of Labrador for a five-year stay. As he made his way through the cold wilderness in search of native trappers, Birdseye had a curious gustatory revelation: Duck, caribou, and fish frozen in the dead cold of midwinter had a better flavor and texture when cooked than those that had been frozen in the milder temperatures of fall and

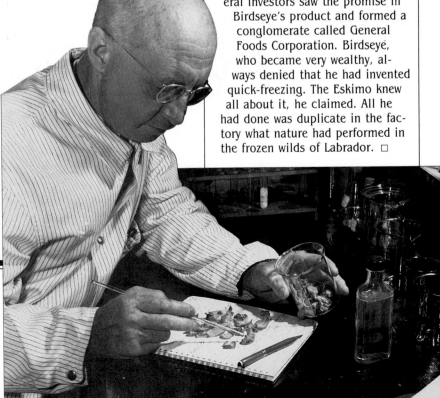

spring. In a flash, he realized this must be connected to the speed with which foods were frozen.

What Birdseye's palate had told him has a scientific explanation. In the freezing process there is a temperature zone during which fluids form extremely large ice crystals. These big crystals press against adjacent food cells and, as the food thaws, cut into the softening cells, allowing the flavor and nutrient-laden fluids to drain out.

It seemed to Birdseye that quick-freezing might be the key to preserving perishables without destroying flavor. Some years after his Labrador stint, he developed a fast-freezing technique that crossed the zone of crystallization so quickly that the large, destructive crystals could not form. In 1924, Birdseye founded the General Seafoods Company to market cartons of fresh fish and rabbit meat that had been quick-frozen between refrigerated metal plates.

At first the company did not prosper—machinery was expensive, and the public had to be convinced that not all frozen foods were mushy and tasteless. But several investors saw the promise in Birdseye's product and formed a conglomerate called General Foods Corporation. Birdseye, who became very wealthy, always denied that he had invented quick-freezing. The Eskimo knew all about it, he claimed. All he had done was duplicate in the factory what nature had performed in the frozen wilds of Labrador. □

Clumsy with kitchen
knives, Josephine
Dickson inspired
her husband, Earle,
to develop the first
Band-Aid.

Cut and Paste

In 1920, minor accidents were a common kitchen occurrence in the New Brunswick, New Jersey, home of Earle and Josephine Dickson. The newly wedded Josephine was a determined but clumsy cook, and Earle, a cotton buyer for the local Johnson & Johnson plant, found himself constantly tending to the little cuts and burns she kept inflicting on herself.

One night, intent on designing a bandage that would "stay in place, be easily applied and still retain its sterility," Dickson placed a broad strip of Johnson & Johnson's surgical tape sticky side up on the table. He unrolled a length of sterile gauze along the middle of the tape, leaving adhesive areas on either side, and then wrapped the whole assembly in crinoline. Whenever she needed it, his accident-prone spouse could cut an appropriate length from the roll, peel off the crinoline, and apply the bandage herself. A co-worker persuaded Dickson to tell company management about his invention, which soon emerged as Johnson & Johnson's Band-Aid. At first, sales were slow. But they soon gained momentum, thanks to a strong endorsement in a drug-gists' magazine and an ad cam-paign that gave free Band-Aids to Boy Scouts and butchers. □

Wired for Sound

William Korzon loved to sing in the bathtub. As he reclined there with the magnificent swell of his own voice reverberating in his ears, Korzon was sure he had real talent. If only he could hear a recording of himself, he said to his cousin Marvin Camras *(above)* one day in 1937, he would perfect the minor flaws and go for the big time.

Camras, then a twenty-one-year-old student in electrical engineering at Armour Institute of Technology in Illinois, saw nothing insurmountable about designing a recording machine for his cousin. He had built radio sets and his own telephone system, and he was familiar with earlier efforts to

make recording machines. He knew, for example, that Danish scientist Valdemar Poulsen had proved in 1898 that sounds could be recorded magnetically. But Camras also knew that the equipment for a Poulsen-style recorder was expensive and the quality of sound was poor.

As he brooded over these problems one day, a solution suddenly came to him: He could use an electromagnetic head to record symmetrically around a wire. Materials would be cheap, and the sound should be clear. Camras put together a prototype wire recorder and whistled "Yankee Doodle" into the microphone. When he rewound

the wire, he heard a garbled noise; but when he played his first wire recording, nothing came forth. The magnetized recording head had wiped away the sound. He tried again, this time demagnetizing the head before rewinding the wire, and the machine faithfully mimicked him. Camras soon had a contract to make his recorders for the United States Navy, which used the devices in training programs to simulate the cacophony of battle.

The wire recorder launched Camras upon a brilliant career in the field of electrical communications. He went on to obtain more than 500 patents for inventions, including the magnetic coatings used on all kinds of recording tape today, high-frequency bias controls, and stereophonic sound. His innovations revolutionized the concept of home sound systems.

For William Korzon, the would-be singer, the wire recorder had provided an unfortunate revelation. After listening to himself warble, he promptly abandoned his musical ambitions. □

Landmark

On a break from his studies at Harvard University, seventeen-year-old Edwin Land was strolling through the bright night of downtown New York City in 1926. As he made his way down Broadway, through a world ablaze with neon billboards, theater marquees, and the blinding swoop of car headlamps, he was suddenly overcome by the light. But he was also inspired, for in that same instant he saw a way to eliminate the glare.

Light waves normally vibrate in several different planes, producing the scattered light that the eye perceives as glare. Land's idea was based on a method of using a filter to channel light waves—or polarize them—into a single plane of vibration. The mechanism had been known since the seventeenth century, but Land was the first to imagine embedding polarizing crystals in a plastic sheet that could be made into lenses. Consumed by his idea, Land took leave from Harvard and began experimenting, often working in a laboratory at Columbia University that he entered secretly through an unlocked window at night. "If you can think of it, you can do it," Land would later say. By 1928, the young inventor had designed, built, and patented the polarizing sheets he had imagined that night on Broadway.

In 1932, he dropped out of Harvard for good and set up the Land-Wheelwright Laboratories, then started the Polaroid Company. As the president, the chairman of the board, and the director of research for Polaroid, Land adhered to a strict policy of never borrowing money and putting the bulk of any profits back into research.

As the years passed, Land seemed to develop an equally strict personal policy of reclusiveness and reticence, refusing most interviews and never initiating or answering correspondence.

Detroit car manufacturers never adopted Land's Polaroid sheets for use in car headlights and windshields as he had hoped. But his company did a good business producing photographic light filters and sunglasses and then picked up some especially lucrative military contracts during World War II. As the war progressed, however, Polaroid found itself short on contracts at a time when the world was awash with military sunglasses. The company was in critical financial shape when, one day in 1943, Land saved the day with another of his visionary scientific flashes.

In Santa Fe on a vacation with his wife, Terre, and their three-year-old daughter, Jennifer, Land had been out taking pictures with Jennifer. The girl had turned to him and asked why she could not see the photographs right away. For Land the question was like a lever that threw open the doors to reveal a scientific field

that was, as he himself described it, "conceptually . . . full-blown." Land's mind pounced on the notion of "instant photography" and, he later recalled, "within the hour the camera, the film and the physical chemistry" had become crystal-clear.

It took him until 1947 to transform his vision into a practical reality. That year, the first Polaroid Land camera, called the Model 95, went on sale at Boston's Jordan Marsh department store the day

after Thanksgiving. It weighed five pounds when loaded and took eight sepia-colored prints per film pack, developing each picture on the spot in sixty seconds.

The instant camera was a success, and by 1958, the Polaroid Corporation was pulling in sales of some $59 million a year. By the time Edwin Land *(below)* retired from Polaroid in 1982, he had received honorary degrees from at least fifteen universities and held 533 U.S. patents. □

Shop till You Drop

Sylvan Goldman had plenty of time and compelling reasons to study the way people shopped for groceries. In 1934, during the depths of the Depression, the veteran Oklahoma grocer acquired several Humpty Dumpty stores—a bankrupt chain of retail grocers in the American South—and faced the daunting challenge of proving his purchase a smart one.

After scrutinizing his customers, Goldman came to a curious conclusion: Women who shopped with a hand-carried basket stopped shopping when the basket got uncomfortably heavy—to Goldman, an unfortunate and premature way for their consuming impulse to end. But the insight also inspired the grocer. In 1936, he had Fred Young, the store handyman, take a folding chair, attach wheels to the ends of its legs, and install two baskets on it. With one bold, deft innovation, Goldman had created the shopping cart.

Full of hope, Goldman placed a few of the new carts in his stores. Nothing happened. Shoppers, slaves to their old habits, ignored the carts and continued to carry their purchases in baskets. Disappointed but undaunted, Goldman tried another dose of homegrown ingenuity on his resistant customers. He hired a few people to act as decoy shoppers, pushing grocery-laden carts around his stores, and had someone offer the carts to customers as they entered. This little encouragement seemed to be all the consumers needed. Soon the shopping cart was off and rolling, and so was Goldman.

He founded the Folding Basket Carrier Corporation to manufacture his wheeled baskets. Then his company began to build a totally new kind of grocery store: the supermarket, whose sprawling expanses had been made feasible by the success of the shopping cart.

When he died in 1984, just one week after the death of Margaret, his wife of fifty-three years, Goldman was said to have left a fortune estimated at more than $400 million to his two sons. Today the shopping cart has a half-ton capacity, about five times more than that of Goldman's original design, and has become an international institution. In fact, the mobile metal cages rank as one of the world's most frequently used four-wheel devices, second only to the automobile. □

Charge It

One night in 1950, Frank McNamara, a tarpaulin company executive, was finishing up a business dinner with clients in a New York City restaurant when he realized he had forgotten his cash. McNamara solved his dilemma by persuading the restaurant owner to wait for his money. But in the heat of the embarrassing crisis he forged a new idea, one that would preclude a reoccurrence of such an event.

After brainstorming with an attorney friend, Ralph Schneider, McNamara introduced on February 28, 1950, the first multipurpose charge card, which he named Diners Club. The idea of credit was hardly new, of course, and oil companies had long exploited the convenience of "courtesy cards" to encourage business at their gas stations. But the Diners Club card marked the first time credit had been offered by an intermediary between seller and buyer. Issued to 200 people—many of them McNamara's friends—and honored at 27 establishments that first year, the card snowballed in popularity.

By 1951, Diners Club had more than 42,000 subscribers paying the annual fee of five dollars and charging more than one million dollars at 330 different businesses. After two years, much of which he spent on the road personally persuading inns and restaurants to accept his card, McNamara left Diners Club to work for a lumber company. But his idea charged on, spawning many imitators and changing forever the way the world shops, travels, and entertains. □

Velvet Hooks

Swiss inventor George de Mestral was hiking through the Alps with his dog one day in 1948 when inspiration stuck to him, literally. As de Mestral was picking out several burdock burs that had nested in his clothes and his dog's fur during their walk, he experienced a curious mental alchemy that connected the burs with another earlier, seemingly unrelated incident.

A few months earlier, de Mestral had been in a similarly annoying situation when a zipper on his wife's dress had jammed. At the time, de Mestral had cursed the zipper and wondered if he could not invent some metal-free substitute. Now, as he pulled stubborn burs from his clothes, he saw in a flash how a substitute might work.

Returning to his home workshop, de Mestral examined one of the burs under a microscope. His intuition had been right on target. The bur, which felt soft when rolled between his fingers, was actually covered with minuscule hooks, which linked up with the loops in any cloth and fur that it touched. The forty-four-year-old inventor envisioned a fastening system of "locking tape," consisting of one cloth strip covered with tiny hooks and another one covered with tiny loops.

But the fastener that had appeared instantly to de Mestral took six years of hard, technically complex work to produce commercially. In his search for a fastening design that would be strong, yet easy to undo and reusable, de Mestral discovered that some 300 loops per square inch were needed and that the loops had to be stiffened with infrared light. But final-

ly, in 1957, he opened the first factory to produce Velcro—*vel*, from velvet, *cro* from the French word *crochet*, a "small hook."

Since its introduction, Velcro has proved indispensable on all sorts of everyday items—clothes, sports equipment, upholstery. Some of the more unusual uses found for de Mestral's invention have been as a sealer in artificial hearts, as an anchoring system for

astronauts in zero-gravity situations, and to help American television talk-show host David Letterman creep up a wall.

George de Mestral received his first patent, for a toy airplane, at the age of twelve; his final invention, a commercially successful asparagus peeler, came in the early 1970s. After an irrepressibly innovative life, he died in 1990 at the age of eighty-two. □

But Can She Type?

In 1951, Betty Nesmith Graham, then simply Bette Nesmith, had recently been hired as an executive secretary at Texas Bank & Trust in Dallas. But all was not well. She found that when she tried to erase errors made with the new electric typewriters, the carbon-ribbon impression left a terrible smudge. Exploiting a correction technique she had used as a part-time sign painter, Graham mixed up a little white tempera paint and carefully camouflaged her flubs.

For five years Graham, a single mother who dearly needed her job, kept her correction fluid a secret. But gradually other secretaries began borrowing the little bottle and brush. By 1956, Graham was running a cottage industry, supplying coworkers with what she called Mistake Out, concocted and bottled in her own kitchen. When IBM declined an offer to market her invention, Graham—who later said her decision was in part due to a dream in which she saw a $700 "invoice blowing in the wind"— tackled the task herself.

By 1980, when Graham died, the Liquid Paper Corporation she had founded was a booming success. Graham's only child, Michael Nesmith—a son from her first marriage and a legend in his own right as a member of the rock group called the Monkees—inherited half of her $50 million estate. The rest went to charities. □

Can Do

Ermal Cleon Fraze got thirsty for a beer one day in 1959 while on a family picnic. When he couldn't find his "church key"—the standard punch-style beer-can opener—he held his beer against a pointed fin on the bumper of his car and managed to bang a hole in the top of the can. Unfortunately, he also managed to soak himself thoroughly. There had to be a better solution, he decided.

After brooding over the problem through the night, Fraze, who had studied engineering at the General Motors Institute, finally had his answer. He would create a pull-tab opener for the top of cans. "I personally did not invent the easy-open can end," Fraze would subsequently explain, after obtaining a patent for his invention in 1963. "People have been working on that since 1800. What I did was develop a method of attaching a tab on the can top."

Indeed, the ingenuity of Fraze's design was in his special attachment rivet, which made the pull-tab practical. The Dayton Reliable Tool and Manufacturing Company, founded and run by Fraze, continued to improve the pull-tab design, eventually creating an environmentally compatible tab that stayed with the can. By the time Fraze died in 1989, his innovation was gracing about 150 billion cans annually as the ubiquitous pop-top, the sudden brainchild of a thirsty inventor. □

Sticky Memos

Art Fry, a product-development researcher for the 3M Company, enjoyed singing in the choir at his St. Paul, Minnesota, church. But almost every Sunday he became frustrated when the scraps of paper he used to mark his hymns fell out during the first service and left him scrambling for his place during the second service. "I don't know whether it was a dull sermon or divine inspiration," Fry said later, describing the Sunday in 1974 when a solution to his problem hit him, "but my mind began to wander and suddenly I thought of an

adhesive that had been discovered years earlier by another 3M scientist, Dr. Spencer Silver."

The "un-glue" invented by Silver was strong enough to hold but easily removed. Fry began testing ways of using it to make a "temporarily permanent" bookmark. Soon he had made the leap to using the adhesive on notepaper, and the idea for Post-it Notes—repositionable memos that could be removed without a trace—was born.

Although 3M officials were dubious about marketing Fry's idea at first, they finally consented to a trial in 1977. It succeeded beyond Fry's wildest dreams, and by 1990

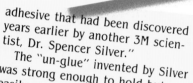

Post-it Notes were one of the five top-selling office-supply products in America. Today the little rectangular memos are a familiar sight everywhere—even in Japan, where the notepads are long and narrow to accommodate vertical writing.

And the staying power of Art Fry's brainchild has begun to generate a kind of Post-it folklore. One resident of South Carolina, for example, wrote 3M in 1989 describing the tenacity of one Post-it that stuck to his front door throughout Hurricane Hugo. "This little piece of paper withstood Hugo whereas eight oak trees in my yard did not." □

Video Visionary

What could one do with America's 60 million television sets, besides turn them on and off? The question nagged at Ralph Baer, a forty-four-year-old engineer with a New Hampshire defense firm. Then, in September 1966, Baer was sitting in a bus terminal in New York when the answer finally came: play games. Seconds later, Baer even envisioned a price tag for his still-formless product: $19.95.

Back at Sanders Associates, his Nashua employer, Baer began to spend all his free time working on the idea. But after a Sanders executive tried a video shooting-gallery game that Baer had devised, the company made the project official. Baer and two colleagues, William Rusch and William Harrison, were assigned to a secret video-game task force.

In April 1972, Baer, Rusch, and Harrison were issued a patent for their "Television Gaming Apparatus and Method." That same year Magnavox—which had licensed the technology from Sanders—brought out "Odyssey," the first home video game package, for $99.95. Baer had miscalculated the price tag by $80, but he had hit a bull's-eye with the overall concept: Video games in 1989 enjoyed sales of more than $10 billion. □

The video game Pro-Soccer, a version of which is shown above, was the brainstorm of Ralph Baer *(left)*.

GRAND DESIGNS

Among the thousands of inventions created by the questing human mind is an elite of enduring innovations. Some of these innovations were so nearly perfect in their initial form that they have survived for centuries without fundamental change. Others have been rediscovered again and again through the ages, as their use has altered, waxed, and waned.

Often, grand designs take the form of a perfecting modification, such as the insertion of matches into a paper cover or the packaging of tea in cup-measure gauze bags—the deft touch of true inventive genius. The majority of humanity's greatest inventions, however, are neither the original object nor the object cleverly refined. They are instead the unplanned offspring of a seminal discovery, the frequently unwitting, intuitive step by an inventor that guides the human future in some unforeseen and unimaginable manner.

Reinventing the Wheel

Although the wheel may well be the pivotal human invention, its inventor and instant of discovery are lost to history. No one knows when an early innovator first noticed that a round thing rolled more easily than a flat thing could be dragged. Some historians believe that, between 4000 and 3500 BC, someone in Mesopotamia—what is now Iraq—must have taken two of the potter's wheels then in common use, linked them with a central axle, and put them to work to transport material ordinarily dragged on a sledge.

So fundamental is the simple device that "to reinvent the wheel" has become a familiar expression for foolhardy redundancy of inventive effort. But, in fact, the wheel has been reinvented many times. The first models were solid, cut from three wooden planks held together by cross struts to make one large board. A knothole served as the hub in these early wheels, since the wood around a knot is tough and wear resistant.

Improved designs appeared in short order. Wheels dating from 3000 BC were fitted with wooden rims studded with iron nails, presumably to make the wheels wear more evenly. By 2000 BC, wooden rims were sometimes replaced by copper strips. At the same time, wheels were getting lighter, thanks to the introduction of spokes in either Mesopotamia or Turkey. By 1500 BC, the Egyptians had begun making all-metal wheels with four flat spokes connecting the hub to the rim. More than a thousand years later, the Romans were making eight-spoked wheels, in which the inside tip of every other spoke attached to opposite sides of the hub, somewhat as bicycle spokes do today. (Further refined by Leonardo da Vinci during the fifteenth century, this structurally improved design was the precursor of wheels used on modern vehicles.)

Although the invention spread widely from its Middle Eastern birthplace, it made no independent appearance in Southeast Asia, sub-Saharan Africa, Australasia, or Polynesia. In the isolated Americas, the wheel was known, but for some reason it was not adopted as a tool. In Mexican ruins dating from AD 300-600, archaeologists have found small pottery figures of animals mounted on small wheels: Someone in the New World invented the wheel but used it only on what seem to be toys. □

Square One

For untold centuries, priests and shamans had seen the random movement of pieces on a patterned board as a way of divining how the hands of gods lay upon the lives of mortals. But, about 5,000 years ago, a nameless ancient must have realized that this same movement, if organized within a set of rules, could turn a tool of divination into a game played on a board.

The oldest board game known dates from around 3000 BC and was uncovered in the 1920s among the ruins of the Mesopotamian city of Ur. The game was played on a richly decorated board, with the movement of each player's seven pieces controlled by the roll of six pyramid-shaped dice—three white and three made of blue lapis lazuli stone. Although its rules are lost, scholars believe it was similar to modern backgammon.

Senat, an Egyptian invention nearly as old, was a racelike game in which a player moved five stone or ivory pieces across a papyrus board. The fast-moving game became a national craze. So compelling was it that King Tutankhamen, among other pharaohs, was buried with his senat board and pieces so that he could continue playing in the afterlife.

The craze did not end with the Egyptian dynasties: Senat contained the seeds of every board game since in which players advance by rolling a die. One of these was pachisi, invented in India in the sixteenth century. The playing board of the Mogul emperor Akbar the Great was his palace courtyard, and the pieces were India's most beautiful women, who vied for a place on Akbar's huge board. This game of moving members of a harem through an Indian palace garden became Ludo in England, and Parcheesi in the United States— once a fad equal to the senat craze that swept ancient Egypt.

Another Egyptian game, called *alquerque,* appeared at least 3,000 years ago; it was a war game in which the other player's pieces were the enemy, to be captured and destroyed. Pharaohs and generals used the outcome to predict the success of their military strategies. Alquerque crossed over into the realm of games after ancient Greeks and Romans adapted it for patrician play. Moving the battlefield to the black squares of a chessboard transformed it into *Les Dames* in the sixteenth century, and, in the seventeenth century, such new features as compulsory capture turned it into the game now known as checkers.

Its military heritage died hard, but the war game survived in other forms, such as Fox and Geese and Officers and Sepoys, in which the game is played between two sides of unequal strength —one fox against thir-teen geese, for example. And as late as 1895, the queen of Madagascar played a checkerslike game called *fanorona* to devise tactics against the invading French army. Her playing must have been off, however, for the French won the war. Doing battle on a board reached its high point with the invention of chess, once believed to have been the work of a fifth-century Hindu in India, or of ancient Persians. (The term *checkmate* comes from the Arabic *al shah mat,* "the king is dead.") But recent archaeological digs in the Soviet Union have discovered ivory chess pieces that predate by at least 300 years the claimed Indian or Persian origins of the game. □

Inlaid with shell, lapis, and red limestone, this board game with playing pieces was used in Mesopotamia in the third millennium BC.

Shades

Legend holds that the first umbrella was invented 3,000 years ago by a Chinese lady to ward off the sun's rays. It quickly became a sign of authority, and only those of royal blood or royal favor were allowed to use an umbrella. The king of Burma took as one of his titles "lord of the great parasol," and only he could use a white umbrella. Other Burmese carried umbrellas whose color reflected the bearer's position in society.

Ancient Egyptians were also great fanciers of umbrellas, which are depicted as a hieroglyphic symbol denoting sovereignty. From Egypt, umbrellas spread into western Africa and the eastern Mediterranean. About 2,000 years ago, historians believe, Greek sailors introduced the device to western Europe, where its primary function was to provide shade—and where it acquired its name from *umbra*, the Latin word for "shadow." But the practical-minded Romans found that their umbrellas could keep off rain as well as sunshine.

Most early umbrellas were made by stretching a fine fabric—decorated cotton or silk, for example—across a large, fixed frame made of wood or whalebone. By the 1700s, however, French inventors had developed the collapsible umbrella, making the device more compact and easier to operate. Still, until the early 1800s a whalebone umbrella weighed more than a large-caliber hunting rifle. By 1826, though, improved materials had reduced the umbrella's weight almost tenfold, to about a pound and a half, and the invention of the metal wire frame in the 1840s reduced it further yet.

Over the years, the umbrella's popularity has risen and fallen with fashion trends and social customs. When the first Indian umbrella arrived in Baltimore in 1772, it

An eighteenth-century English painting entitled *The Battle of the Umbrellas* pokes fun at awkward bumblers with their bumbershoots.

frightened townsfolk, caused horses to bolt, and drew a hail of stones from children. The town watch had to restore order. In England during the 1700s, carrying an umbrella marked a commoner: It meant the bearer had no carriage. Later, no proper British gentleman would be seen in public without one, no matter what the weather. But for years after umbrella-toting Prime Minister Neville Chamberlain's 1938 meeting with Adolf Hitler in Munich, at which it was agreed that Germany would take over a sizable portion of Czechoslovakia, the umbrella was a symbol of spineless appeasement. □

Pointless

In 1849, New York inventor Walter Hunt found himself fifteen dollars in debt and made a deal with his creditor. The debt would be forgiven, and Hunt would get $400, in exchange for the rights to any useful device he could shape from an old piece of wire. A brilliant innovator, Hunt had developed a number of designs, including a repeating rifle and the sewing machine, although he had forgone patenting the latter *(page 22)*. He readily accepted his creditor's challenge. Three hours later, Hunt had invented the modern safety pin.

In fact, Hunt was not the first to see a safety pin in a length of wire. The first improvement upon the straight pin had appeared in central Europe about 3,000 years earlier, when bronze pins were bent into a U shape and the point secured into a hook fashioned into the wire. But this model left the point still exposed.

By the sixth century BC, Etruscans were making safer pins than the one patented by Hunt. These had a built-in spring, formed by making a coil in the wire, and a shield to hide the point and protect the wearer from being pricked. Etruscan safety pins, on display in museums throughout Europe, were elaborately crafted from gold with lions and other figures, and they were apparently intended to be seen. Called *fibulas,* they were probably worn by Greek and Roman women to fasten their robes on the shoulder and upper arm.

As clothing became more complex, the demand for such decorative clasps increased. One fourteenth-century French princess had 12,000 of the expensive fasteners. The hard-to-get objects were often hoarded by women of the Middle Ages. To discourage hoarding, British authorities allowed pin makers to sell their wares only on certain days, for which women set aside their extra change—pin money, as they came to call their small allowances. □

Pressing Engagement

Of all household chores, ironing may be the most hated, for few activities combine strenuous effort with such drudgery. A century and a half ago, however, it was worse. Many buildings were equipped with gaslights, and numerous inventors designed gas-fired clothes irons, which, while reducing wrinkles, also leaked, caught fire, and even exploded.

Before that hazardous development, ironing had changed very little over the 2,400 years of its existence. Greeks in the fourth century BC devised a way of using a hot metal rod, similar to a rolling pin, to put pleats in their linen robes. Two hundred years later, the Romans used a metal mallet to beat the wrinkles out of their clothes. Beyond that, the history of irons has largely been one of heavy metal objects heated to a dangerously high temperature, wielded by exhausted servants and spouses.

In 1903, the burden was made lighter by California power-plant supervisor—and part-time inventor—Earl Richardson. Since electricity was used almost exclusively for lighting, few power companies then ran their generators around the clock. Richardson asked his employers to produce electricity for twenty-four hours one day a week, on Tuesdays. Then he persuaded a few housewives to try his new invention, a lighter-weight iron that was heated electrically.

The experiment was a success. Advised by his wife that the first model was too hot in the middle and not hot enough at the tip, Richardson went on to create the successful Hotpoint iron in 1905. And the power company, encouraged by ironing Tuesdays, moved to provide household current day and night—a practice that was eventually adopted nationwide. □

A HOMEMAKER'S GODSEND, the Hotpoint electric iron *(below)* and others like it replaced heavy, cumbersome flatirons in the early twentieth century. Their use was promoted by utility companies, which sold the irons to customers to increase the use of electricity. The strategy worked. Soon only the light bulb exceeded the iron as a consumer of household electricity.

Buttoned Up

Buttons have been around since at least the third millennium BC, and they have scarcely changed in 5,000 years. Even the earliest button yet discovered, a carved mollusk shell found in the ruins at Mohenjo-Daro in the Indus Valley of India, has two holes pierced in it so that it could be sewn to a garment. But, for nearly 4,000 years, buttons were merely decorative. No one thought to invent the buttonhole until the thirteenth century, when European tailors paired the button and buttonhole as an alternative to pins, which damaged fine fabrics and were easily lost or misplaced.

The novel fastener soon had Europe's aristocracy seized by button mania. Fourteenth- and fifteenth-century clothing was often slit from neck to ankle just so the rift could be fastened with buttons and holes. It was not uncommon for arm and leg seams to be closed with buttons as well. Everywhere in Europe, buttons were used to signal the wearer's wealth and station.

This aristocratic lineage produced an odd tailoring tradition: Men's clothes button from right to left, women's from left to right. By studying portraits through the ages, fashion historians have traced this practice back to the fifteenth century, when buttons were still expensive. Men, who usually dressed themselves and were predominantly right-handed, preferred that their buttons close from right to left. But women who could afford buttons usually had dressing maids as well. Because the servants faced their mistresses to dress them, and were also mostly right-handed, they found it easier if the button and buttonhole were reversed. The convention, like the button itself, still exists today. □

The button mania that seized European fashion in the Middle Ages is reflected in the amply adorned clothing of Anne Boleyn, Henry VIII's second wife.

Meal Tines

As inseparable as the knife, fork, and spoon may seem today, the fork was a latecomer to the table, finding its way into most homes only in the nineteenth century. The implement, originally bearing two prongs, was invented by Tuscan craftsmen in the eleventh century, but it was an object of ridicule for much of its existence. Even in its Italian birthplace, clergy denounced the utensil, proclaiming that only human fingers, created by God, were worthy to touch the food that God provided. A century later, a Venetian fork user was rebuked for showing an "excessive sign of refinement." When the woman died several days later from the plague, priests called her death divine punishment—for using a fork.

Since Roman times, the refined way to eat had been to use the thumb and first two fingers. The less polite used all five fingers. As late as the 1530s, a popular European etiquette manual reminded its readers that three fingers were proper eating tools, indicating that the fork had not yet come into vogue. The main use of the two-pronged implements was as large serving forks.

The fork's acceptance was still some centuries away when, at least among the upper classes, it became a common practice to use a spoon or the sharp point of a knife, rather than fingers, to pick up food. But the pronged utensil remained a strange object to most. Cautioned one seventeenth-century book of manners: "Do not try to eat soup with a fork." Finally, in pre-revolutionary France, the fork came into its own when high-living aristocrats adopted four-tined forks, partly to distance themselves further from commoners. □

This seventeenth-century silver fork was considered an "excess refinement" in its day. So rare were forks in daily use that genteel travelers had to carry their own.

Slurpies

About the only difference between today's postage stamp and the British one issued in 1840 is the cost. The world's first stamp cost a penny and revolutionized postal services worldwide. Until then, postal charges had been based on the number of pages in a letter and the distance it traveled, and the tariff was collected not from the sender but from the recipient.

In 1837, British educator Rowland Hill proposed a single tariff, based on weight, prepaid by means of "labels" glued to the mail. Public support for this idea was strong, and, on May 6, 1840, the government introduced a gum-backed, lick-and-stick stamp that quickly became known as the penny black *(above)*. It was soon followed by the tuppence blue. But the ease with which the penny black could be altered to obliterate the cancellation mark doomed it. In 1841, it was replaced by the penny red, designed and printed with an eye to thwarting fraud. □

Writing Sticks

About seven inches long and a quarter inch in diameter, the modern pencil is not a very impressive-looking device. But from the time of its invention two centuries ago it has reigned as the champion of writing instruments. In the United States alone, several billion pencils are made and sold per year, each of them capable of scribing the equivalent of a 45,000-word book.

Today's pencil is little changed from the design that Nicholas-Jacques Conté *(below, left)* invented in 1795 at the request of the French war minister. At the time, France was at war with Britain, and its supplies of high-quality English graphite had been cut off. Conté began work on a substitute.

Until the advent of graphite, lead was used as a rudimentary marking device, but it never appeared in pencils. In Conté's day, German manufacturers of a crude pencil used a process, developed in the seventeenth century, that mixed powdered graphite with sulfur and resins to produce a material that could be formed into sticks that did not disintegrate. These markers, still known as leads, were encased in wood or clamped in a mechanical holder.

Because France had meager supplies of the high-quality graphite required, Conté added clay as an extender. He formed a thick paste from powdered graphite, clay, and water and shaped it in long, thin rectangular molds. After the paste dried, Conté fired it in a kiln. The resulting graphite sticks proved to be among the best writing implements yet invented. Even better, Conté found that he could make the sticks harder or softer by adding or subtracting clay from the starting mixture. The softer the resulting pencil lead, the darker its line.

Modern pencil factories still use Conté's basic method for making graphite sticks of varying hardness. The best pencil graphite comes from Mexico, Sri Lanka, and Madagascar, and German clay is the best binder. To make wooden pencils, manufacturers have modified Conté's process, making six grooves in two slabs of wood, inserting leads, and gluing the slabs together in a kind of sandwich, from which single pencils are then cut. Most of the wood for modern pencils is aromatic cedar, harvested from trees that sprouted in the mountains of California and southern Oregon about the time that Jacques Conté completed his timeless design. □

Fall Guy

There have been various kinds of hoists and lifts since ancient times. Indeed, the pyramid builders of Egypt used an early variant of the elevator. But the lifts were not considered altogether safe for people—until 1854. In May of that year, at New York City's Crystal Palace Fair, Elisha Graves Otis, a forty-two-year-old tinkerer from Vermont, changed elevators, and the look of American cities, forever. Otis, bearded and wearing a top hat, stood on an elevator platform full of boxes and barrels as it was raised forty feet in the air by a thick rope cable. Then, suddenly, an assistant took an axe and chopped through the rope. The platform jerked downward, the crowd gasped, a woman screamed—and nothing happened. "All safe, gentlemen, all safe," declared an unruffled Otis, with a tip of his hat.

The demonstration was more showmanship than risk, for the inventor was never in danger. The lift was fitted with a safety mechanism Otis had developed at the Yonkers bedframe factory where he worked. The device was triggered automatically by a heavy wagon spring connected to the thick cable that lifted the elevator. As long as the cable was taut, the spring remained compressed; but if the cable went slack—as it would when severed—the spring snapped out and forced two iron bars into

notches cut in the vertical guide rails of the elevator shaft, locking the elevator in place.

Three years after his dramatic demonstration, Elisha Otis installed the world's first passenger elevator in the five-story E. V. Haughwout china and glassware store in New York City. This steam-powered hoist traveled forty feet per minute and could carry 1,000 pounds. But the implications of his safety mechanism went far beyond the installation of elevators in existing Manhattan buildings. Without passenger elevators, the height of buildings had been limited to the stairs people were willing to climb, about five stories. With a safe, mechanical alternative to stairways, the skyscraper was not too far behind. □

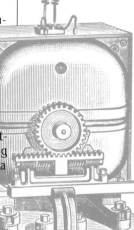

The safety elevator's inventor, Elisha Graves Otis, is flanked by two of his creations. The elevator of the 1930s, proudly displayed by its operators (*above, left*), succeeded the Otis electric elevator (*right*) of the 1890s.

OTIS
RIC ELEVATOR

On a Roll

In the early 1990s, a novel kind of roller skating called blading became something of an international fitness craze. Named for the trademarked Rollerblade design, blading looks like ice skating on wheels. The boot, made of the hard, durable plastic called polyurethane, could easily be that of an ice-hockey skate, but instead of a metal blade on the bottom, there are three or four polyurethane wheels set in a straight line. Stridently modern, the skates are in fact a resurgence of an old idea: The original roller skates, invented in eighteenth-century Holland, also placed the wheels in line.

Belgian manufacturer Joseph Merlin, the first recorded roller-skate maker, attempted to publicize his wares in 1760 by blading into a prestigious London ball while playing a priceless violin. Like others who had tried the new diversion, Merlin was not adept at maneuvering—or stopping. He crashed into a huge mirror worth more than £500 and was severely injured—as was the reputation of the in-line roller skate.

It took a hundred years and the inventive and publicity skills of Massachusetts furniture salesman James Plimpton for the roller skate to regain its popularity in a different form. Plimpton had taken up ice skating on the advice of his doctor. When winter ended he tried roller skating, but found he was no better than Merlin at controlling his movements.

Plimpton realized that the key to maneuvering a wheeled skate was having some way of rocking

Like the first roller skate, this 1963 version carries its wheels in line. Above, skating enthusiasts of the 1930s race on the familiar, four-wheel skate that eclipsed the original.

the boot from side to side, thus varying the pressure on the wheels to produce turns and stops. He accomplished this by placing two pairs of metal wheels under the heel and toe of a metal footplate, and a hard rubber ball between the rollers and the plate. The skate, able to rock slightly, was remarkably easy to control. He patented his guidable skate in 1863.

Several years later, he invented the roller rink, a place where people could socialize while getting exercise and, not incidentally, rent his skates. The roller rink was a success, though not entirely for the skating: It provided a socially acceptable, chaste opportunity for women to meet men. By 1876, the forty-eight-year-old Plimpton controlled a skating empire stretching across the United States and Europe. But his monopoly endured only as long as his patent; when it expired, others began to compete.

Meanwhile, skating with the original, in-line design had persisted as an art form. An opera, *Le Prophète*, included a simulated ice-skating scene that was performed on stage in roller skates. In 1849, composer Paul Taglioni wrote a ballet, *Winter Pastimes; or, The Skaters*, that used wheel-bladed skates to represent an ice-skating scene. Jackson Haines, an American ballet master who was also an accomplished ice skater, performed on roller skates in 1864 and proved to be so captivating that his techniques became the foundation of today's international style of artistic skating, on wheels and on ice. □

Slippery Success

In 1859, Robert Augustus Chesebrough believed he had seen the future, and it was grim. The twenty-two-year-old chemist owned a small kerosene-refining business in New York that seemed headed for trouble: Large oil fields had been discovered in Pennsylvania, and Chesebrough feared that major refiners would drive him out of business. A practical man, he decided to see if he could put his chemistry skills to work in the budding petroleum industry. Out in the oil fields, he heard men complain about a waxy substance called rod wax that collected on the oil pumps. An annoying material, it had one redeeming feature. According to the oil workers, rod wax soothed and healed the many cuts and bruises sustained by their rough-working hands.

Intrigued, Chesebrough collected a sample of the substance and took it back to his Brooklyn laboratory. Over the next eleven years, he purified the slippery residue, searching for the essence of its healing powers.

He acted as his own guinea pig, cutting and burning his fingers to test various preparations. By 1870, he had found an effective salve that helped his wounds heal quickly and without infection. He called the petroleum-based ointment Vaseline *(below, left)* and touted it as a substitute for existing salves—which, since they were made of animal fat and vegetable oils, tended to turn rancid.

To promote his colorless, odorless, and tasteless healing balm, Chesebrough traveled across upstate New York, passing out one-ounce jars of Vaseline. Orders poured in, and soon, so did endorsements. Admiral Robert Peary, for one, took Vaseline with him on his arctic expedition because it did not freeze at forty degrees below zero. Vaseline began to be used as a balm for burn victims. And, over the years, customers have found thousands of other uses for the substance: as fishing bait, to soften baseball mitts and protect car battery terminals from corrosion, to prevent lip chapping, to remove makeup, and as a cosmetic cream.

None of this would have surprised Chesebrough, who died in 1933 at age ninety-seven. A true believer in the limitless powers of his invention, he swallowed a spoonful of Vaseline every day for the last thirty-five years of his life, and, when ill, he covered himself from end to end with the versatile product that he had discovered in supposedly useless rod wax. □

Muffed Opportunity

Winter in Farmington, Maine, is hard on any exposed human ear, but it was especially bad for Chester Greenwood, who seemed to have the coldest ears in town. Cold weather painfully transformed them from a healthy pink to a frozen blue. In 1873, his parents gave the fifteen-year-old a pair of ice skates for Christmas, and he dutifully set about finding a way to use them without losing his ears.

He fashioned two loops out of baling wire and asked his grandmother to sew a piece of beaver fur on one side and black velvet on the side that would sit against his ears. She then sewed a piece of wire connecting the loops to Chester's bowler hat. That day when he went skating, his ears re-

mained a healthy pink color. The enterprising lad had beaten winter.

Before long, the people of Farmington wanted their own pair of "earflaps," and the women in the Greenwood family were spending much of their time making what eventually became known as Greenwood's Champion Ear Protectors. Chester improved his original design by connecting the muffs with springy flat steel, which kept the muffs pressed onto the ears. When he patented the design in 1877, he said: "I believe perfection has been reached."

Eventually, Greenwood invented a machine to manufacture earmuffs, and Farmington became the earmuff capital of the world. When Greenwood died in 1937, the factory there was operating twenty-four hours a day turning out millions of earmuffs based on his original design.

Although Greenwood's earmuff plant has long been closed, December 21—the first day of winter—is still celebrated as Chester Greenwood Day in Maine. Farmington hosts a parade, complete with a coldest-ears contest. □

With his ears snugly shielded from the frigid winters of his native Maine, Chester Greenwood stands by a placard advertising his "Champion Ear Protectors."

Tubing

In 1892, Dr. Washington Wentworth Sheffield, a New London, Connecticut, dentist, packed his popular Creme Dentifrice into a flexible metal tube, thus creating the first tube of toothpaste. Until then, dental cream had come in porcelain jars, and family members would scoop it up with their toothbrushes. The more sanitary tube toothpaste was a big success, and sales of the dental cream that Sheffield and his son had developed in the mid-1850s skyrocketed. But soon the Sheffield Dentifrice Company started making flexible metal tubes for other products as well, and, over time, the containers themselves became the most important part of the company's business. □

Heat Seal

The thermos was originally invented in 1892 to store supercold liquid air at low temperatures. Sir James Dewar, a Scottish chemist, told his German glassblower, Reinhold Burger, to create a special double-walled glass vessel by attaching a small flask inside a slightly larger one. The air between the two would be drawn out completely before the flasks were sealed together at the top. Since heat cannot cross a vacuum, this would isolate the cold material inside from its warmer surroundings. For extra protection, the vacuum flask, as Dewar called it, was coated inside and out with a thin reflective layer of silver to retard the transfer of heat by radiation. Such vessels used in low-temperature research today are called Dewars.

Burger, the glassblower, realized that the vacuum worked both ways—if it kept heat out, it would keep it in. He and two business partners built a metal casing to protect the fragile twin-walled flask and designed a lid to seal it. (An American company later replaced the silver coating with nickel.) The three patented their consumer version of Dewar's invention in 1903, and they held a contest to name the product. Thermos, which means "heat" in Greek, was the winning entry. The term spread throughout the world and became so commonplace that in 1970 a judge ruled it could no longer be considered a trademark. □

Sir James Dewar's skeptical mother-in-law knitted a woolen cozy to keep her grandson's milk warm—insurance against the possible failure of her son-in-law's vacuum flask.

The Whisker King

In 1894, King Camp Gillette was a bottle cap salesman and a frustrated inventor who admired his boss, William Painter, creator of the Crown Cork, a throwaway bottle cap. One day the magnanimous Painter offered the thirty-nine-year-old Gillette some crucial advice: "Why don't you try to think of something like the Crown Cork which, when once used, is thrown away, and the customer keeps coming back for more?"

Gillette took Painter's words to heart. Over the next few months, he ranged through the alphabet trying to think of a product that would be both useful and disposable. Then, on a hot summer day in 1895, Gillette was shaving with a cumbersome razor that badly needed sharpening, when inspiration struck. "As I stood there with the razor in my hand," he recounted later, "the Gillette razor was born—in that moment I saw it all, more with the rapidity of a dream than by the slow process of reasoning. The way the blade could be held in a holder; then came the idea of sharpening the two opposite edges on the thin piece of steel; the clamping plates for the blade, and a handle easily disposed between the two edges of the blade. All this came more in pictures than in constant thought, as though the razor were a finished thing and held before my eyes." Gillette wrote his wife, then out of town on a visit, "I've got it! Our fortune is made!"

But envisioning a safety razor and building one were two very different matters. Gillette spent

By saving time, money, and facial skin, the Gillette safety razor quickly converted millions of American men into dedicated customers.

the next six years trying to make a practical disposable blade, and he finally succeeded with the help of William Nickerson, a highly regarded mechanical engineer. Along the way to inventing the razor blade, Nickerson had to invent machines for hardening and sharpening thin steel. In 1904, Gillette was granted a patent for his safety razor.

To obtain further backing for his new invention, Gillette persuaded a wealthy friend to back him, then gave away the new device to friends. He promoted the safety razor as a saver of both time and money. Early advertisements proclaimed: "Saves $52.00 each year. Saves 15 days time each year."

The first year of sales, 1903, Gillette sold a paltry 51 razors and 168 blades. The year after, however, sales totaled 90,000 razors and 124,000 blades. By 1908, the Gillette Safety Razor Company pro-

duced 300,000 razors and 14 million blades. Five dollars bought a holder and 20 blades packed into a velvet-lined, full-leather case. Twenty replacement blades cost a dollar. The company's big break came with World War I, when the U.S. Army ordered 4.2 million Gillette safety razors for the troops in

Europe. Those soldiers came back dedicated Gillette customers. Since then, the company founded by Gillette and its competitors have vied in making razors slimmer, safer, cheaper, prettier, and even more expendable, trying to improve on King Gillette's near-perfect idea. □

Drink

Coca-Cola

Delicious and Refreshing

Boxcars

When Coca-Cola first became available in bottles in 1899, customers tended to buy one or two at a time, usually to drink right away. But in 1923, New Orleans bottler A. B. Freeman hit upon a new marketing ploy: six bottles in a handy cardboard carton. The idea was a smashing success, and people flocked to carry Coke home to their refrigerators six at a time. But, while still used for soft drinks, Freeman's invention soon had a new identity: Almost anywhere in the world today, a six-pack means beer. □

DRINK Coca-Cola

SERVE ICE-COLD

DELICIOUS AND REFRESHING

The six-bottle carton
– at home

Flaky Foods

In the 1890s, Dr. John Harvey Kellogg and his younger brother William Keith—who styled himself W. K.—spent a good deal of time experimenting in the kitchen of Michigan's world-famous Battle Creek Sanitarium, which specialized in ailments ranging from nervousness to indigestion. W. K., the health spa's business manager, and John, the superintendent and chief surgeon, were strict vegetarians and sought continually for new ways to make the sanitarium's meatless fare as interesting as possible by creating new dishes.

One day in 1894, the brothers had boiled a batch of wheat when they were both called away unexpectedly. They did not remember their unfinished experiment until the next day, when, returning to the kitchen, they found the wheat covered by mold. Nevertheless, they decided to run it through rollers just to see what would happen. In earlier experiments along similar lines, rolling the boiled wheat had produced a sticky, gummy, and unappetizing dough. But this time, rolling produced an amazing change: Each wheat berry turned into a flake. When toasted in an oven, the flakes yielded a crunchy and, allowing for the mold, tasty food. The Kelloggs had discovered, accidentally, the process of "tempering" cooked cereal to equalize the amount of water in the batch—the secret of successful flaking.

Eventually, the brothers overcame the mold problem by storing boiled grain in tin-lined bins. The sanitarium patients loved the new cereal, which came in wheat and

corn flavors, though the latter was judged too tough and too bland.

In 1906, W. K. decided to go into the breakfast-flake business and bought rights to the invention from his older brother, who wanted nothing to do with such a venture. W. K. also did some further research on the unpopular corn flake and found that corn grits mixed with tiny bits of malt, salt, and sugar made a delightful flake after all. He called the dish Kellogg's Toasted Corn Flakes, a product destined to become the world's most popular breakfast cereal.

Soon, orders for Corn Flakes were coming into the Kellogg factory faster than they could be filled. Kellogg started an aggressive advertising campaign for Corn

One Taste of Kellogg's Makes the Whole World Kin

There is a flavor to Kellogg's Toasted Corn Flakes that everybody recognizes instantly and likes from the start. Kellogg's is enjoyed by every age and in every station. Always fresh and ready to serve. At all grocers—and at hotels, restaurants and lunchrooms in individual cartons—clean and crisp.

Look for this Signature
W. K. Kellogg

Flakes, and it was not long before 4,000 cases a day were rolling out of the Battle Creek factory. A disastrous fire in 1907 almost did the company in, but Kellogg persevered to build what is now the world's largest producer of breakfast cereal.

The Kellogg brothers' culinary experiments also inadvertently produced some keen competition. In another part of Battle Creek, a young cereal company was doing a booming business largely because its founder, Charles W. Post, had been at the right place at the right time. He had been a patient at the sanitarium and had enjoyed the healthful food served there so much that he decided to enter the field himself. In 1894, the year the Kelloggs stumbled upon their grain flakes, he had created Postum, a hot health beverage that did well during the cold part of the year. He was trying to think of a product to sell during the warm months, when patients at the sanitarium began extolling the virtues of cold breakfast cereals. Post set to work in his own kitchen and developed tiny nuggets of processed wheat and malted barley. He called them Grape Nuts. □

Zip!

In 1891, tired of bending over to lace up his high boots, chubby Whitcomb Judson invented the first slide fastener. Two years later he obtained a patent on an improved version. The device was difficult to fabricate, however, and very unreliable. Brought to the brink of bankruptcy, Judson formed a partnership with Harry Earle and "Colonel" Lewis Walker, who hired an engineer by the name of Gideon Sundback to try to save the fastener.

It took the twenty-six-year-old Swede several years, but, by 1912, Sundback had invented a new slide fastener and the machinery with which to manufacture it. Sundback's design consisted of two rows of alternating metal teeth. Each tooth had a protrusion on one side and a cavity on the other, so that the protrusion of one tooth would fit snugly into the cavity of its partner. The teeth were brought together and separated by means of a Y-shaped slide. Vastly superior to earlier models, the new fastener was reliable and easy to make.

Leery from their experience with earlier Judson fasteners, clothing manufacturers at first stayed away from the new hookless one. Sales trickled in until 1917, when 24,000 slide fasteners were used in sailors' money belts. Then, in 1923, the fastener got its big break. One of the rubber giants, B. F. Goodrich Company, began fitting their galoshes with the hookless fastener. The move did more than bring success to Walker's Hookless Fastener Company— it gave the device a name. Describing how easily the boots could be donned or doffed, a Goodrich executive said, "Zip 'er up or zip 'er down." The slide fastener has been known as a zipper ever since. □

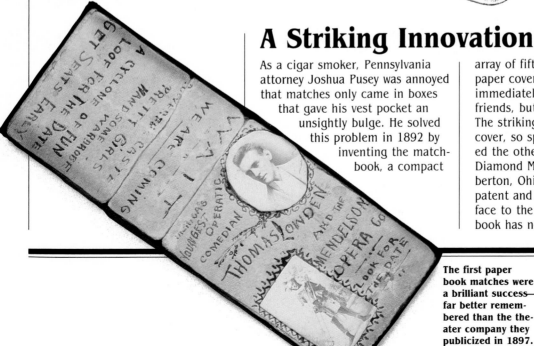

The awkwardness of the first slide fastener nearly bankrupted its portly inventor, Whitcomb Judson. Subsequent redesign put zip in its workings—and in its name.

A Striking Innovation

As a cigar smoker, Pennsylvania attorney Joshua Pusey was annoyed that matches only came in boxes that gave his vest pocket an unsightly bulge. He solved this problem in 1892 by inventing the matchbook, a compact array of fifty matches held in a paper cover. These first books were immediately popular among his friends, but they had one problem: The striking surface was inside the cover, so sparks occasionally ignited the other matches. In 1895, the Diamond Match Company of Barberton, Ohio, bought Pusey's patent and moved the striking surface to the outside. The matchbook has not changed since. □

The first paper book matches were a brilliant success— far better remembered than the theater company they publicized in 1897.

On the Ball

In 1888, American leather tanner John Loud patented a new type of marking device that used an inked roller ball to write on leather. This original ballpoint pen was never produced, however, nor were the following 350 or so ballpoint designs patented by other inventors since: The pens invariably leaked or clogged.

Half a century after Loud's attempt, two Hungarian brothers tried their hand at developing a functional ballpoint. One of the brothers, Ladislas Biro, was a newspaper editor who hated filling fountain pens and cleaning ink smudges. He was also tired of tearing newsprint with a fountain pen's sharp point. Georg, his brother, was a chemist. Together, the two set out to create improved inks and a better pen to put them in.

By 1938, they had made a few ballpoint pens, and while on a seaside vacation they demonstrated one to an elderly gentleman they had met on the beach. He turned out to be Augustine Justo, the president of Argentina, and he invited the brothers to set up their pen factory in his country. When World War II broke out in Europe, the Biro brothers fled to Argentina, found several investors to finance their invention, and by 1943 were turning out pens.

Because the Biro brothers' creation depended on gravity to feed ink to the roller ball, it worked only when held straight up. Ladislas and Georg went back to the drawing board and came up with an improved ink tube that worked on capillary action: The roller ball acted like a sponge, drawing just enough ink from the tube to wet a piece of paper, and the pen could be held at an angle. This was a vast improvement. For a time, the Biro ballpoint enjoyed great popularity in Great Britain, where high-flying Royal Air Force and Army Air Corps crews needed a pen that, unlike ordinary fountain pens, did not leak in the low pressures found at high altitudes. But in peacetime, the ballpoints were poor sellers, and the Biro brothers went broke.

Meanwhile, an enterprising fifty-four-year-old Chicago salesman named Milton Reynolds had seen the Biro pens in stores in Argentina. Back in the United States, he set up a factory and put his first pens on sale at Gimbels department store in fall 1945. Soon, along with several competitors, he was selling the ballpoints by the millions. But, again, the bubble burst: The pens still clogged and the ink still smudged.

One of the casualties was Los Angeles chemist Fran Seech, who lost his job when the ballpoint pen company he worked for went under. He continued to work on new combinations of inks and roller balls at home. In 1949, he met Patrick Frawley, a young importer-exporter, who was so impressed with Seech's work that he opened a pen factory and began marketing the inventor's design, a retractable ballpoint tip with no-smear ink. Dubbed the Paper Mate, the pen was a huge success. Within a few years, several hundred million had been sold.

At about the same time, Frenchman Marcel Bich became interested in ballpoint pen design. For two years, working independently, he analyzed existing ballpoints in minute detail, often using a microscope. Finally, in 1952, Bich produced a clear-barreled, smooth-writing, nonleaky—and above all, inexpensive—model he called the Bic. But the original inventors have not been forgotten: In England, a ballpoint pen is still called a biro. □

Dust Off

Despite brooms and carpet sweepers, life until the the early twentieth century was dusty indeed. New devices aimed at making it less so seemed to do little more than move dust around from one spot to another. For example, in 1901 an American inventor on a visit to England demonstrated a carpet cleaner that worked by blowing dust off the floor into a box—and everywhere else.

British inventor Herbert Cecil Booth was not impressed when he saw the cleaner in action, for he had given the matter of cleaning dusty floors much thought and knew blowing was not the answer. Several days after the demonstration, he thought he had a solution. "I tried the experiment of sucking with my mouth against the back of a plush seat in a restaurant in Victoria Street," he recalled. So much dirt came out that he almost choked. In principle, at least, he had invented the vacuum cleaner.

Satisfied on the experimental side, Booth built and patented a working vacuum cleaner and start-ed a cleaning service. The device was so enormous that it rested on a horse-drawn cart. An 800-foot hose connecting the gas-powered vacuum machine to the dust nozzle was pulled through a window to clean the interior of a house. It became popular among upper-class women to host tea parties while vacuum cleaning was in progress, just to demonstrate the wonderful invention.

Meanwhile, across the ocean in Canton, Ohio, James Murray Spangler was having health problems—severe coughing brought on by his work. The fifty-nine-year-old Spangler had once been a successful inventor but now was employed as a janitor in Canton's Folwell Building. Sweeping the building's carpets was aggravating his asthma so badly that he decided to invent a better cleaning tool.

As an interested observer by the name of Frank G. Hoover recounted later, Spangler "worked on it during the day when his time was his own. He started with an old soap box, sealed the cracks

In the Bag

Thomas Sullivan was a New York importer who wanted to find a less expensive way of sending tea samples to prospective customers. The standard method of shipping such samples was to put them in small tins, but these containers were becoming too expensive for Sullivan's limited trade. In 1904, he got the idea of putting small amounts of tea in compact Chinese silk bags, which saved him money without making the product seem cheap. But his customers misunderstood. Instead of removing the tea from the carrying bag, they put the sample, bag and all, into the boiling teapot. Without quite intending to, Sullivan had invented the tea bag. □

with adhesive tape; he made a roller brush, they say, by stapling goat bristles to a piece of broom handle. And he cut out a better fan from an old stovepipe. The fan motor provided the power and a pillow case served as a bag. The new machine worked so well that Murray ceased to worry about his job. . . . The Folwell Building and its acres of rugs became a huge laboratory to Murray Spangler.''

Spangler eventually refined and began building his portable machines. He sold one to a cousin in Ohio: Mrs. William H. Hoover, Frank's mother. The Hoover family had been in the saddlery business, but, with the coming of the automobile, they were looking for something new. In 1908, William Hoover bought the manufacturing rights from Spangler, and in 1948, Frank ascended to the presidency of the thriving Hoover Vacuum Cleaner Company. By then, Hoover had long been a household word as well as a common name for the vacuum cleaners. Even today, in Great Britain, where the device was born, the common word for vacuuming is hoovering. □

Seeking relief from asthma, James Murray Spangler *(above, left)* **invented the portable vacuum cleaner. Seeking wealth, William H. Hoover** *(above, right)* **made it a commercial success.**

Until 1944, when they adopted their present rectangular shape, Lipton tea bags were shaped like the 1920s sack shown above, sewn from huge reels of gauze *(below)*.

Dixie Land

In America at the turn of the century, thirsty citizens drank from public tin dippers hanging in barrels of water. Hugh Moore, a young Kansan living in Boston, thought the practice unsanitary and went into business selling spring water at places along the trolley line. For just a penny, the trolley rider could get a drink of water in a disposable paper cup that Moore's brother-in-law, Lawrence Luellen, had created. But Moore had few customers: Nobody wanted to pay for something they could get free.

Moore's break came from his home state of Kansas. Dodge City's health officer was conducting a crusade against public drinking dippers, calling them a health hazard that spread disease. In 1909, he succeeded in getting Kansas to ban dippers, even those aboard railroad cars crossing the state. Moore was quick to realize that he had been trying to sell the wrong thing—the water instead of the cup. He persuaded the railroads to install paper-cup dispensers on trains, and Moore's Health Kups

Xuccess Xtory

Chester Floyd Carlson was a twenty-nine-year-old physicist-turned-patent lawyer, frustrated by the number of documents his work forced him to copy. It was the mid-1930s, and copying a document was a tedious task. Photographing and photostating were the only methods available then, and both were costly and time-consuming. Carlson was convinced that there had to be a better way.

After attacking the problem on his own for three years, Carlson asked his friend Otto Kornei, an engineer, for help. They set up a laboratory in the back of a beauty parlor in the Astoria section of Queens, New York, and, working together, the men developed a process they named xerography, from the Greek words meaning "dry writing." They made their first copy on October 22, 1938. It read: "10.-22.-38 ASTORIA."

The process itself was fairly simple, and the versatile copying machines today employ the same basic principle as the first one built behind the Queens beauty parlor. Carlson and Kornei coated a metal plate with sulfur, a material that holds a static charge in the dark but loses the charge when exposed to light. With the lights out, Kornei charged ◊

were soon selling briskly. Eventually, thinking Health Kups needed a punchier name, he picked one from a doll company named Dixie.

Other states copied Kansas, especially after a professor at Lafayette College published a list of germs he had collected from glasses in a public school system. Moore, attentive to publicity for his cups, began a feverish advertising campaign. "Influenza Sits on the Brim of the Common Drinking Cup," the ads' heading warned. "Avoid the common drinking cup as if it were the plague itself." □

The first xerographic copy *(above)* made by Chester Floyd Carlson *(right)* shows the date and location of the experiment that led to an office revolution.

the sulfur-coated sheet with static electricity by rubbing it with a silk handkerchief, then wrote his dateline message on a glass slide, which he placed on the charged plate. When he shone a light on it, the plate discharged its electricity everywhere *except* where letters on the glass slide blocked the light. Next, the men sprinkled the coated plate with powdered ink, which stuck to the still-charged areas. Finally, they pressed a piece of ordinary paper against the plate and the image transferred to the paper. Heating the paper fixed the message, preventing it from smearing or fading.

It took another six years for Carlson to make a machine that would do mechanically what he and Kornei had done by hand. And then came the hard part: finding a company that would invest money to produce their xerography device. Carlson contacted dozens of companies, to little effect. One private research organization, the Battelle Memorial Institute in Columbus, Ohio, provided a small amount of research money, but not enough to make the many improvements Carlson knew were possible.

Help came from John Dressauer, the research director of the Haloid Company, a small manufacturer of photographic paper in Rochester, New York. Dressauer had read an article on xerography that Carlson had written for the magazine *Radio News*. Impressed, he persuaded his company to purchase the rights to Carlson's copier, and on October 22, 1948—just ten years after the first successful experiment in Astoria—the company introduced its new machine, called a Xerox. While not an immediate success, it sold well enough to warrant further development.

In 1959, the Haloid Company became the Xerox Corporation and introduced the fully automatic Model 914 copier. It weighed 648 pounds, made 7 copies a minute, and cost $29,500. Realizing that few companies could afford to buy the copier, Xerox offered a rental plan: $95 per month, 2,000 free copies, and a nickel a copy after that—and free repair service. The Standard Pressed Steel Company of Boston rented the first 914, and employees there made over 100,000 copies the first month alone. Today, the company that grew from Carlson's 1938 invention makes more copies just testing its machines than the entire world made in 1960. □

CURIOUS PATENTS

Machine for Making Pills.

Above a door at the Commerce Department headquarters in Washington, D.C., are inscribed these words of Abraham Lincoln, president and patent holder: "The patent system added the fuel of interest to the fire of genius." Since the late eighteenth century, when the United States government began granting patents, the system has indeed fueled a blaze of creative genius by assuring the right of inventors to profit from their creations.

Patents may be granted for almost anything that has no precedent. But many patents do more than protect new ideas: They reflect the human preoccupations of their times. Thus, some patents are concerned with killing or coddling various animals. Others focus on the endless fight against crime. Still others deal with aspects of that peculiarly human object of affection, the self.

No matter how grand or quaint the invention, it represents the fruit of a creative moment. For breakthroughs and tinkerings alike, the inventors' sketches, descriptions, and carefully crafted models, such as the one shown above, testify to ideas whose time, at least in the view of the creators, has come.

Better Mousetraps

"To build a better mousetrap" has come to evoke that combination of inspiration and profitability that inventors strive to achieve. In fact, the mousetrap is a device that has been created again and again. With almost pathological fervor, inventors have pursued the destructive little rodents since ancient times.

The historical record suggests that humans around the world have been destroying mice for thousands of years and trapping them at least since the time of ancient Greece. Indeed, the Greeks used the phrase "a mouse in a pickle jar" to describe someone in trouble.

The first American mousetrap patent was issued in 1838, for a simple, spring-operated snapping device much like the conventional mousetrap that is still sold today. Since then, no fewer than four thousand inventors have beaten a path to the door of the U.S. Patent Office, seeking recognition for their own refinements and variations on the popular theme of anti-rodent technology.

Few mousetrap designers achieve

Asahel A. Hotchkiss of Sharon, Connecticut, patented this better mousetrap in 1870. Capable of assassinating five mice at a whack, the trap uses baited chambers around its circular base to lure vermin to their death. When a mouse sticks its head through one of the holes to retrieve the bait, the trap springs a U-shaped metal garrote, which flips up and strangles the creature.

#101,620: 1870

great wealth; some of the patented traps never even make it to market. Still, the economic possibilities are enticing. Americans spend about $350 million each year to hire professional rodent exterminators and purchase some twenty million traditional snap-type traps. The U.S. Patent Office examines 50 to 100 mousetrap patent applications a year and finds 65 to 70 percent of the proposed devices sufficiently innovative to be eligible for patent protection.

Many of these better mousetraps are uncompromisingly lethal. The quest for an efficient means of killing unwanted mice seems to

have tapped an inexhaustible vein of deadly ingenuity. Inventors have patented traps that poison, asphyxiate, drown, electrocute, gas, guillotine, and fatally stress mice.

Others have concocted nonlethal trapping methods. Many so-called humane traps, which generally cost more money than their traditional mouse-killing cousins, feature escape-proof containers that lure the mouse in and confine it until the human trapper decides the creature's fate. But the humane traps do not sell nearly so well as the lethal ones, suggesting that, to most people, the only good mouse is still a dead one. □

All in One Plan

High-tech mousing that not only kills but crushes and incinerates the victim is offered in a trap devised by Texan Ted M. Moss. His enclosed apparatus lures a doomed rodent into a cylindrical chamber with bait. An electric eye senses the presence of the mouse and actuates a spring-driven vertical harpoon that spears the creature on the spot. Once dead, the mouse is crushed between two flat metal plates to a thickness of about three-sixteenths of an inch and incinerated by an electric coil. The trap then automatically places another morsel in the bait chamber and resets itself to harpoon the next small intruder. □

#4,669,216: 1987

Jarring Maze

#1,618,513: 1927

An ordinary Mason jar becomes a bewildering labyrinth for mice with the addition of a device invented by Charles W. Coghill. The trapper baits the jar and fastens Coghill's attachment to its open mouth. As a mouse crawls into the jar through the attachment's funnel-shaped passageway, it pushes under a hinged wire gate, which falls shut behind the animal. Seeing light at the end of the funnel, the mouse proceeds into the jar. Then, wanting to escape, it returns to the funnel, finds the opening above the closed gate, and exits— back into the jar. As Coghill explained in his patent application, "The mouse when making efforts to escape will be perplexed at finding escape to be impossible when it appears to be easy." □

Gas Chamber

Two Illinois inventors, Andrew J. Pratscher and Philip J. Andres IV, patented a mousetrap "with gas injector to effectively, continually and rapidly exterminate rodents and other animal pests with carbon dioxide or other gases in a reliable, efficient and safe manner." The device traps a mouse or a rat in a baited entrance chamber, which seals itself and rotates into the trap's interior. There, the victim is gassed and dropped into a disposal chamber. □

#4,741,121: 1988

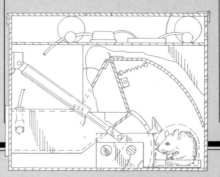

Mousepaper

Samuel T. Hughes of Alabama patented a device designed to capture, not kill, mice. It consists of a box with a hole at either end, inside which bait is suspended from the ceiling. The floor is a pad of adhesive sheets, installed sticky side up. Entering through one of the holes, the mouse sticks to the top sheet. The trapper then lifts away the box and peels off the top sheet, wrapping the rodent, which may still be alive, for disposal— and exposing the sticky surface of the second sheet. □

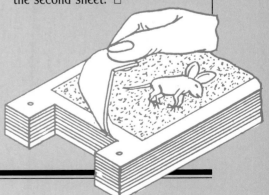

#2,962,836: 1960

Dewormer

Inventors have not limited their trapping talents to the rodent population: They have also moved against an enemy within. Indianan Alpheus Myers patented a ''Trap for Removing Tapeworms from the Stomach and Intestines,'' a hollow metal cylinder about three-quarters of an inch long with a cord attached to one end. Filled with bait and swallowed by the patient—''after a fast of suitable duration to make the worm hungry''—the trap entices the hungry worm to insert its head through an opening in the side. This triggers a spring-loaded interior wall to snap shut and seize the creature, allowing it to be withdrawn with the cord. □

#11,942: 1854

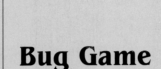

#798,825: 1905

Bug Game

Danish inventor Rasmus Petersen was living in New Jersey when he patented a gun for bagging very small game: insects. When the bug hunter pulls the trigger of Petersen's gun, a sliding rod flies forward from the barrel, causing a pair of catchers at the muzzle to spring open, then quickly snap shut, imprisoning or killing an insect caught between them. Petersen specified that the gun's fly catchers should be edged ''with a rim of rubber or some soft material'' to prevent damage when stalking prey on walls and ceilings. □

Net Gain

Swedish-born New Yorker Carl E. K. Andersson invented a double net for catching more than one fly at a time. As he put it, ''No care is necessary in handling the net to avoid the escape of the insects caught while catching others,'' adding that ordinarily ''the insects must be removed at once,'' since they otherwise might be injured as the net whipped around catching other flies. Andersson's fly catcher consists of a long, thin dip net with a smaller net, open at the bottom, nested in its mouth. By employing a sweeping motion, the user snags insects in the small net and also sets up a rush of air to force them through its bottom into the larger net, where they are held securely while the net is used to trap more of their fellows. □

#404,946: 1889

In 1790, the U.S. Congress passed, and George Washington signed, the first federal patent law, ''An Act to promote the Progress of useful Arts.'' Just 3 patents were issued that year, but a century later the annual number had climbed to more than 24,000; by 1990, it had soared to 90,000. In all, some 5 million U.S. patents have been issued over the years.

Flea Pit

Rudolph Bosshard of Los Angeles invented a trap "by means of which fleas can be readily caught either by directly bringing the trap into position where the flea jumps or by leaving the trap in a place infested by fleas, so that the fleas may accidentally come thereupon and be entrapped." The trap, he wrote, could be placed in a bed or in clothing "or anywhere else where the fleas are liable to be." His invention is a thin, hollow disk with one side perforated with numerous small holes, and the other side smeared on its inner surface with a sticky substance. Fleas jumping in through the holes in the perforated side get stuck and cannot jump out. The trap can be taken apart to dispose of captured fleas and to renew the supply of the sticky substance. □

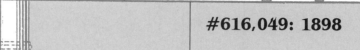

#616,049: 1898

Bug Blaster

For sleepers tired of being bugged and bitten in bed, New York inventor Frank M. Archer devised an electric bedbug exterminator that uses pairs of electrified contacts "arranged so that the bugs in moving about will close the circuit through their own bodies." With these contacts at strategic locations on a bed, Archer declared, "currents of electricity will be sent through the bodies of the bugs, which will either kill them or startle them, so that they will leave the bedstead." The device should be turned off after every use, he further explained, to avoid startling the human sleeper. □

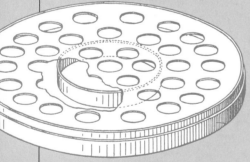

#761,195: 1904

This flytrap model, patented in 1872 by Massachusetts inventors Addison M. Chapel and James G. Hubbard, uses a clockwork to turn a baited wheel marked with indentations. The wheel traps intruding flies and shunts them into a holding cage for subsequent disposal.

#133,354: 1872

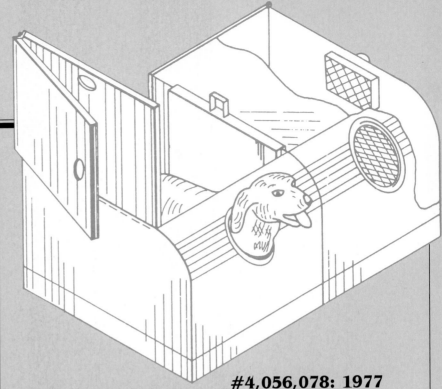

Pet Toll

Though dedicated to the destruction of such pests as mice and fleas, inventors have been much preoccupied with the comfort, health, and safety of creatures that share the human experience, as pets or livestock. To improve communications between dog and cat owners and their pets, for example, Louisiana inventor Fred M. Adams devised an alarm activated by scratching. Designed to fasten to the inside or outside of any door, it offers pets a scratching surface on a vertical board with a bell clapper attached to the top end. When the action of the scratching animal's claws sets the board in motion, the clapper strikes a bell, tolling a signal that tells owners where their animal is—and to come open the door. □

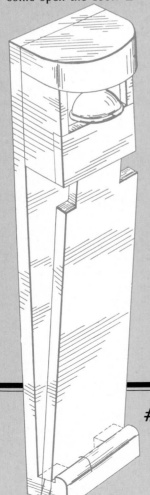

#2,655,122: 1953

Whirladog

After showering in one compartment of the pet washer patented by Brooklynites Clem and Antoinette Blafford, a dog can move into an adjacent compartment and automatically activate hot-air blowers to dry its fur. By putting the two compartments side by side within a single enclosure, the Blaffords' invention permits a wet dog to pass directly from shower to

#4,056,078: 1977

drying stall without stepping outside. This is an important feature, according to the inventors, because a damp canine "generally shakes itself vigorously to remove the water from its coat and this results in the animal handler, the adjacent floor, walls and any others who may be in the vicinity being the recipient of the water shed by the animal." □

Chic Chix

#730,918: 1903

Andrew Jackson, Jr., of Tennessee patented hen goggles, "designed for fowls so that they may be protected from other fowls that might attempt to peck them." With two lenses mounted on an adjustable frame, the eye protectors can be tightened or enlarged to fit birds of different sizes. One section of the two-piece frame wraps around the chicken's head while the other arches over the top of the beak to hold the lenses in place. □

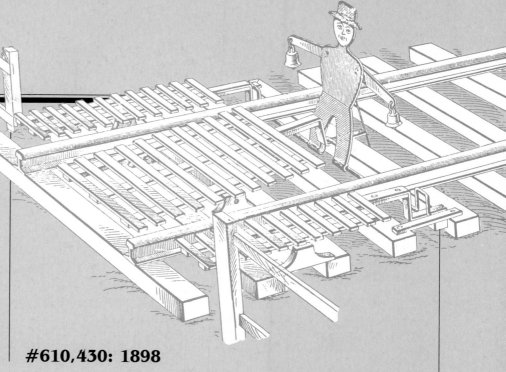

Scarecow

To drive off livestock wandering onto railroad tracks, Charles G. Cozine of Kentucky invented a kind of cutout "scarecow" that combines the jangling of bells with a pop-up figure that springs from the track bed to startle stray animals. Cozine's device employs a painted human figure clutching a bell at the end of each outstretched arm. The figure lies flat between the rails until an animal's footfall on a triggering platform causes the cutout to leap up, ringing its bells. □

#610,430: 1898

Hangs a Tail

A clamp patented by Vermont inventors Thomas Andrus and Napoleon Prior is designed to hold a dairy cow's tail aloft during milking, "so that it will be impossible to switch it into the milk-pail, or switch it in the face of the milker." The triangular clamp is suspended from a long wire attached to overhead members of the stall and hangs down alongside the cow's flank. By clasping the tip of her tail, the clamp inhibits unwanted flicks but leaves the animal "a certain amount of liberty to move her tail." □

To help horses beat summer heat, Philadelphia inventor Edward T. Balch patented this sunshade, which, wrote Balch, "protects the animal from the heat of the sun and at the same time creates a current of air above the head," discouraging flying pests.

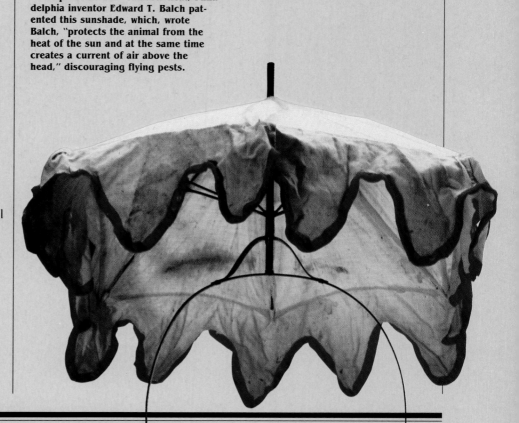

#99,282: 1870

#255,233: 1882

#4,827,666: 1989

Veg Heads

Inventors may also patent changes made to living things. Sometimes they reach into the genetic blueprint of a plant or an animal to create a unique descendant; more often, though, they merely alter the way something looks. For example, Richard Tweddell III, a playful inventor from Cincinnati, has developed a process that changes the face of vegetables.

A toy designer by trade, Tweddell holds the patent on a line of plastic molds he calls VegiForms, designed to give such common, easily grown produce as squash, cucumbers, and zucchini an extraordinary appearance. His interest in changing the shapes of growing vegetables originated when he was a college student doing summer farm work. Noticing that the growth of vegetables was influenced even by such small obstacles as pebbles and tufts of grass, he began experimenting to see whether this tendency could be used to mold a vegetable's shape. When he slipped bottles over baby zucchini,

squash, and other produce still growing on the vine, the vegetables gradually assumed the shapes of the containers.

Tweddell then moved on to specially made molds of clear plastic and started coaxing vegetables into more complex configurations. Some of his VegiForms squeeze growing cucumbers into geometric shapes that provide heart- and diamond-shaped slices. Another lets waggish gardeners grow yellow squash that look like ears of corn. Others impart elflike faces to pumpkins, squash, small pickling cucumbers, and other vegetables.

Tweddell has also made celebrity veggies—eggplants with the face of Elvis Presley, Ronald Reagan squash, Margaret Thatcher zucchini—but cannot market the molds because of the large licensing fees involved. For the less famous, Tweddell will work from photographs and produce six so-called vanity molds so that buyers can grow their faces as VegiForms in their own gardens. □

Endless Luck

Starting not with an invention but a lucky discovery in a domestic flower bed, Ellis H. Dearing of Oklahoma cultivated and patented a previously unknown strain of water clover. Clovers ordinarily grow with three leaves, and those with four leaves are so rarely encountered that they are used as good-luck charms. But Dearing's variety has distinctive clusters of four leaves on each stem, which repeat from generation to generation: a perpetual four-leaf clover. □

#3,730 (plant): 1975

Weak Beans

Most commercially cultivated beans are harvested by mechanical pickers that pull leaves, stems, and other debris from the plants along with the edible bean pods. But the harder the bean pluckers pull, the more waste material they shake loose, and the more costly it becomes to separate the morsels from the mess. Seeking a solution, Oregon inventor Roy Schulbach developed two green-bean plants, identified as AgS1 and AgS2, bred specifically for a low pod detachment force. Barely a pound of effort is needed to yank the patented beans off their stalks. □

Made Mouse

With the progress of genetic engineering technology, scientists have refined techniques for transplanting genes, which carry hereditary instructions, from one creature to another—in effect, inventing new breeds of animals with specific traits. In 1987, the U.S. Patent Office announced that it would begin accepting applications for patents on genetically engineered animals. The following year, a team of Harvard University medical researchers led by Philip Lederer and Timothy Stewart made scientific history by applying to patent a new mammal: a better mouse.

The so-called Harvard mouse might not agree that its re-engineered genetic blueprint is an improvement on the original. Designed for use in research laboratories, the animal was modified when still a one-celled embryo to be highly susceptible to cancer. By studying generations of the tumor-prone rodents, scientists will be able to learn more about the hereditary aspects of the disease.

But patenting the Harvard mouse set off a storm of public debate. Farmers worried about the cost of genetically engineered cows and pigs, fretting that they might have to pay patent royalties every time a patented animal gave birth to offspring with the same genetic traits. Ecologists warned of unforeseen consequences if genetically engineered creatures escaped into the environment to compete or interbreed with naturally occurring animals. Activists from the animal-rights movement charged that some forms of genetic manip-ulation would constitute cruelty and abuse. Congress responded by enacting a temporary ban on animal patents, suspending action on nearly one hundred pending applications. The prohibition against patenting animals has since expired, but the issue remains a contentious one for scientists and politicians alike—and the hapless Harvard mice, still used in research, remain the only mammals to have been patented in the United States. □

#4,736,866: 1988

Faceplate

Although some inventors dabble with creations involving other organisms, more have been fascinated by the human species—with how people decorate, groom, and clean themselves, what they do for exercise, and how they protect themselves from one another. Not even the seemingly simple procedure of applying lipstick is free from this penchant for improvement. Women could put on their lipstick with greater precision, for example, by using the lip stencil patented by Marie L. Helehan of Montana. The user opens the stencil, which folds flat for easy carrying, holds it against the mouth, and follows its outline when applying lipstick. "The described device may be made in different sizes to fit different sizes of mouths," the inventor notes, "and with different edge contours to outline different types of lips." □

#2,117,061: 1938

Chew Brush

Noting "the reluctance on the part of busy people to take the time to execute a thorough dental hygiene program," a California inventor named Dennis G. Oates developed an inconspicuous alternative: the "mouthbrush." Unlike a traditional toothbrush, which the user grasps by a handle and inserts partially into the mouth, the handleless mouthbrush is a cluster of bristles small enough to fit entirely inside the mouth. Projecting in all directions from a lozenge-shaped plastic core, the bristles massage the gums and probe between the teeth as the brush is "chewed like chewing gum." □

#4,748,709: 1988

Bathing Suit

Milwaukee inventor James Franklin King patented an inflatable, waterproof bathing bag for those without access to "ordinary bath conveniences." The bather can either pour water into the bag before entering or add water through a nozzle after closing the bag with a drawstring at the neck. Scrubbing is achieved by "alternate crouching and rising in the bag or by rolling with the same upon a bed or floor." □

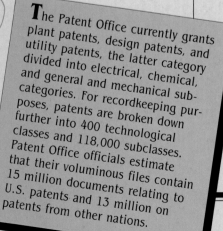

The Patent Office currently grants plant patents, design patents, and utility patents, the latter category divided into electrical, chemical, and general and mechanical subcategories. For recordkeeping purposes, patents are broken down further into 400 technological classes and 118,000 subclasses. Patent Office officials estimate that their voluminous files contain 15 million documents relating to U.S. patents and 13 million on patents from other nations.

#1,066,121: 1913

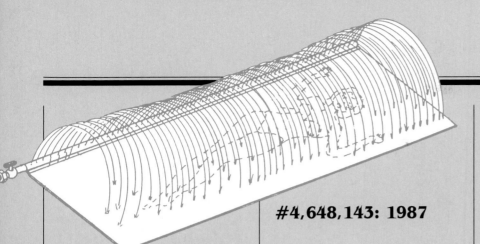

Body Baster

#4,648,143: 1987

Sunbathers brought to a broil can cool off with a combination tanning mat and sprinkler invented by Connie C. and Roddy P. Breaux of Louisiana. A garden hose is connected to the open end of a tubular conduit that runs up one side of the mat. When a valve is opened, water flows into this conduit, which is pierced along its length by a series of small holes. Spray from the holes bastes the sizzling sun worshiper with a cool, refreshing mist. □

Toe by Toe

Ohio inventor Russell E. Greathouse noticed that when sunbathers lie on their backs, their feet pivot apart, exposing the inner thighs and calves to more sunlight than the rest of the legs. To rectify this problem, Greathouse patented a toe holder that keeps the feet together. A simple pair of connected rings that slip over the sunbather's big toes, its use, according to the inventor, produces "a relatively uniform burning effect." The holder also features a touch of elegance: a small hole between the toes for a decorative flower. □

#3,712,271: 1973

Nose Probe

Frank J. Daley of Connecticut devised an implement for cleaning the nostrils of infant children without impeding free breathing or damaging sensitive tissue. Molded of firm but flexible rubber, Daley's tool, shown below in an original and a modified form, consists of a stem with leaf-shaped protrusions that scrape the nostril clean as the invention is inserted, rotated, and withdrawn. A bulge in the shaft keeps the tool from probing too far into a baby's nose. □

A wearable ear trumpet won a patent for New York inventor Frank M. Blodgett. The outsize hearing aid was hooked behind the ear, while the tapered, rubber-covered tip, equipped with amplifiers, was inserted into the ear.

#2,096,162: 1937

#439,099: 1890

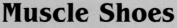

Bound to Boogie

Dancing partners can keep their act together—and make it sparkle—with the help of special battery-powered belts invented by Josephine Infante of Brooklyn. Each partner wears one of the belts buckled around the waist. The dancing couple is connected by a pair of elastic cords, clipped to hooks mounted on the sides of their belts just above the hips. As the partners dance, the intermittent tension exerted by their gyrating bodies on the elastic cords triggers a battery switch, causing colored lights on the belts to flash rhythmically on and off. □

#3,458,188: 1969

Gym Chair

An armchair patented by Joseph F. Sterling of Florida combines relaxation with exercise, offering the option of working selected muscle groups with the aid of devices concealed inside the body of the chair. The built-in exercise equipment includes a resilient handgrip at the end of each arm, a frame that folds out between the front legs, and spring devices attached to handles that protrude from the arms and headrest. According to the inventor, the chair provides an attractive piece of furniture "in which the individual can have an exercise program without moving from his chair or from the front of the television set or other entertainment in his home." □

Muscle Shoes

New Zealander Percy Adolphus Vaile obtained a patent from the United States for "an improved article of footwear to be worn by persons when engaging in physical-culture exercises or for other purposes and especially designed to develop the muscles of the legs, ankles, and feet." The special shoe that Vaile described in his patent application features a metal lining fitted inside the leather to reinforce the toe to carry a metal holder for small dumbbells and other weights of varying size. □

#757,983: 1904

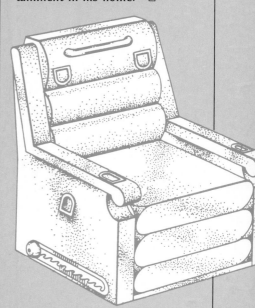

#4,921,247: 1990

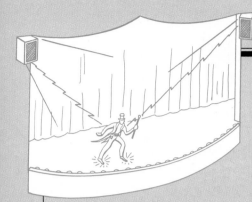

Tapping Electronics

A tap shoe invented by Charles E. Medler and Terry C. McInturff of North Carolina can amplify the sound of a tap dance performance and even convert the tapping into a variety of musical effects. Each time the shoe strikes the floor, pickups inside the hollow taps produce an electrical signal that travels up a leg wire to a small pocket transmitter, which relays the impulse to a receiver-amplifier. The signals are then passed directly to loudspeakers as amplified tapping, or fed through a synthesizer to produce musical notes or other sounds. □

#4,660,305: 1987

Hip Hip

Noting the pleasure and health benefits that dancers derive from "rapid and supple gyrations of the body," New Jersey inventor Anthony A. Haroski created a "hip-toss ball game" to provide the same exercise. Haroski's apparatus consists of a belt worn around the player's waist, a shallow basket supported by a pair of rods projecting from the front of the belt, and a ball on a cord hanging near the rim of the basket. The object of the game is to use hip movement to swing the ball into the air and catch it in the basket. □

#3,610,622: 1971

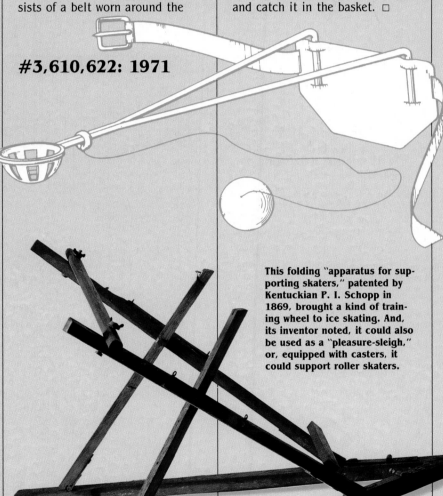

This folding "apparatus for supporting skaters," patented by Kentuckian P. I. Schopp in 1869, brought a kind of training wheel to ice skating. And, its inventor noted, it could also be used as a "pleasure-sleigh," or, equipped with casters, it could support roller skaters.

#86,699: 1869

Bike Spike

As a painful deterrent to bicycle thievery, Adolph A. Neubaurer of New Jersey invented a bicycle seat equipped with a retractable spike. Upon parking the vehicle, the owner flips a switch to release the spike, which pokes up through the seat, ready to do grievous injury to a careless bicycle thief. □

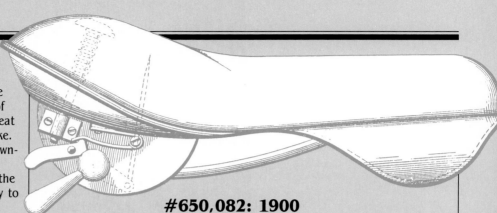

#650,082: 1900

The Pits

Ohio inventor William Carr's patent added yet another pitfall to the risks of burglary. His invention uses a concealed chamber that is located beneath the premises and covered by a pair of trapdoors set flush with the real floor. A burglar stepping on the doors plummets into the trap, where his weight on the floor of the chamber activates a system of rods or chains that pulls the trapdoor shut, preventing the thief's escape. □

Sleeper

Drawing on the technology used to tranquilize animals and knock them out without killing them, Max L. Robinett of Kentucky obtained a patent on "a system which will disable a robber as same attempts to flee from the scene of the crime so as to permit apprehension of the robber at the scene." Designed for installation in the walls just inside a bank's doorway, Robinett's invention fires needle-sharp projectiles treated with a knockout chemical. □

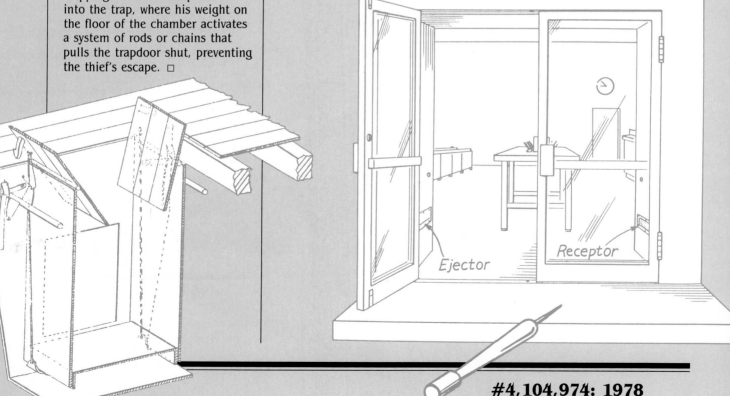

Ejector

Receptor

#4,104,974: 1978

#77,582: 1868

116

Pickpocket Piranha

Although it looks and feels like an ordinary wallet, the device invented by Watson Franklin Curry of St. Louis is intended to catch pickpockets red-handed. The bogus wallet is tethered to the inside of a pocket with a string and safety pin. When a pickpocket grabs the wallet and yanks the string, four concealed fishhooks pop up and bite into the thief's hand. Because the device also has the effect of tying the victim and the presumably enraged criminal together, Curry cautioned that "the trap is intended to be used by law enforcement officers" trolling for pickpockets and thieves. □

#2,522,606: 1950

A bootjack that doubles as a burglar alarm was modeled by New Jersey inventor F. C. Goffin for his 1858 patent. Ordinarily, the device was used as a brace for pulling off boots. But when it was placed by a door, its footrest worked as an alarm system. The treadle could be cocked to snap open and bang against the door if an intruder tried to enter.

Autopus

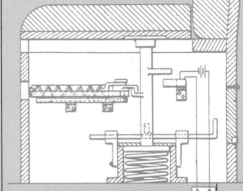

#1,368,543: 1921

Auto thieves find themselves in the clutches of their victims with Philadelphia inventor Thomas N. Burghart's tenacious device. An unauthorized person's weight on the driver's seat of the car trips a spring mechanism, causing a pair of pincerlike cuffs to shoot out from under the seat and seize the thief's legs in an escape-proof grip. At the same time, a loud alarm sounds to alert passersby that a criminal has been caught in the car trap. □

#19,844: 1858

Backtrack

A curious shoe patented by Maryland inventor Cecil Slemp has a specially designed sole with "heel and toe positions reversed so that the wearer leaves tracks indicating a travel direction opposite to the actual direction of travel." Slemp intended his invention to be both a novelty item and a serious piece of military gear "particularly useful in combat conditions on patrol or any secret mission that requires confusing the enemy." □

#3,823,494: 1974

Hidden Heel

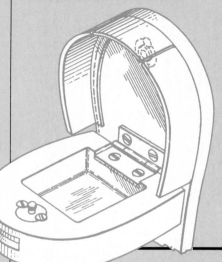

Shoes with secret compartments in the heels are standbys of smuggling and espionage, but inventor Lawrence E. Bodkin of Florida described his hollow-heeled shoe as an innocent device for hiding "a few coins for lunch money for school children, bus tokens, door keys, small emergency funds, train tickets, and the like." What makes Bodkin's shoe different is that the hollow heel swings downward on a hinge, permitting concealed items to be retrieved without dismantling the heel or removing the shoe. □

#2,897,609: 1959

Shootcase

Noting that a traveler "is exceedingly helpless against the unexpected demand of a highwayman," Oscar V. Hargrave of Massachusetts patented a "means of self defense which can be carried, aimed and fired without attracting attention until the very moment of the firing." His invention takes the form of a "hand bag, grip, dress suit case or other article of luggage, with a fire-arm." A hole in one end of the luggage is aligned with the barrel of a pistol mounted in the case, fired by operating a lever with a ring located just under the handle of the bag. "If, now, a footpad or other dangerous character suddenly appears and threatens his life," wrote Hargrave, the user "simply introduces his finger in the ring, directs the suit case toward the miscreant's legs, and pulls upon the ring." □

United States patent law imposes no restrictions regarding who is allowed to apply for a patent on a new and useful invention. The inventor may be of any age and need not be a citizen or a resident of the United States. A patent application filed from prison is perfectly acceptable, and an application may even be filed in the name of a deceased or mentally impaired inventor. If such an application is approved, it is the inventor, not the guardian, executor, or filing attorney, whose name appears at the top of the patent document.

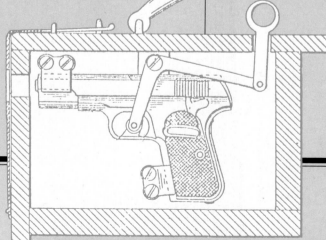

#1,381,301: 1921

Camou Cape

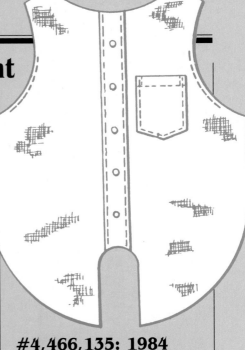

#4,466,135: 1984

#4,792,471: 1988

Hunters wishing to hide themselves more effectively as they stalk wild animals in the woods can use the camouflage strip patented by Ben R. Lee of Alabama. A long, narrow panel of material designed to be wrapped in many different arrangements around the user's body, the invention is studded with fasteners, some to keep it in place, others for affixing pieces of artificial foliage to disguise the outline of the hunter's body. □

Solid Investment

A person wearing the garment patented by Virginia inventor Edward A. Coppage, Jr., appears to be wearing an ordinary dress shirt. In fact, the wearer's vital areas are secretly bulletproofed by a light-fabric vest that, with front buttons and pockets, is intended to blend into the dress shirt it covers. Both the front and back panels of Coppage's vestlike shirt contain hidden pockets concealing pads of du Pont Kevlar or some other bulletproof material. Fasteners located at the neck, shoulders, and sides connect the front and back halves of the shirt, and the pads can be removed from their pockets for laundering. □

#178,243: 1876

A burglar alarm was patented by John P. Kislingbury of Rochester, New York, using this scale model. When the ordinary door bolts are withdrawn by an intruder, the device automatically double-bolts the door and sounds a loud bell alarm. "It is effective," its inventor wrote, "against burglars and tramps."

Twiddler

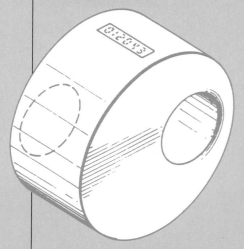

#4,227,342: 1980

While all patents are utilitarian, some are less so than others, filling niches so small as to seem trivial and suggesting that necessity is not always the true mother of an invention. A novel creation of Washington, D.C., inventor Horace A. Knowles offers a case in point. Designed as "an amusing, rotating device that is powered by rotation of the two thumbs," the invention features one hole for each thumb and is small enough to be rotated without colliding with the other fingers of the user's hands. It also has a counter that totes up the number of revolutions. The purpose of the object? In the inventor's words, to "improve the pleasure of thumb twiddling for even those highly skilled in the art." □

Snow Machine

Canadian inventors Ralph R. and Judy A. Maerz received a patent on a tool for making "aesthetically pleasing and aerodynamically sound" spherical snowballs without touching the snow with one's hands or mittens. Resembling a pair of pliers with a hemispherical cup at each of the gripping surfaces, the snowball maker has slots in each cup so that excess snow is expelled as the user works the handles to bring the two hemispheres together and mold a snowball between them. □

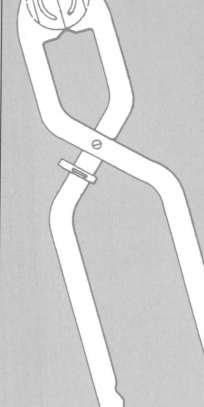

Some Locket Gum

A locket invented by Christopher W. Robertson of Tennessee was meant to be worn as a piece of jewelry on a chain around the neck, just like a traditional locket containing a loved one's picture or some other personal item. But Robertson's locket is not for just any memento. It consists of two hinged sections, each padded on the inside and fitted with a concave piece of crystal that serves as an anticorrosive lining. "Chewing gum may thus be carried conveniently upon the person," the inventor wrote in his patent application, "and is not left around carelessly to become dirty or to fall into the hands of persons to whom it does not belong." □

#395,515: 1889

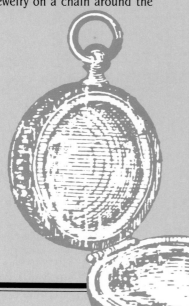

#4,859,167: 1989

Pulsating Pumps

Seattle inventors Mart F. Irving and William R. Duncan described their illuminated shoe heel as a safety device that helps to make the wearer more visible on darkened streets. Consisting of a transparent heel with an electric light source inside, the invention turns on when the wearer's weight is on the shoe and turns off when the foot is lifted, causing the heels to flicker as the wearer walks, providing "an interesting effect when worn to parties and the like." □

#2,941,315: 1960

A one-piece suite of furniture was modeled by Valparaiso, Indiana, inventor Edwin J. Green for his patent of a "combined wardrobe, bedstead, and table," shown here in both its table and bedstead modes.

#224,679: 1880

#3,809,520: 1974

Hot Scoop

When dishing out hard, frozen ice cream, it is desirable to use a scoop that is warmed in some way—usually by letting the scoop soak in a container of water between servings—so that its edge will cut more easily through the cold confection. An alternative method patented by California inventors Richard B. Wilk and Jack J. Hill uses a fluid circulation system to warm the bowl of the scoop, a technique, they noted, that avoids the hazard of heating scoops by electrical means. In their design, hot water from an ordinary tap circulates through a tube into the handle of the scoop and flows through a hollow space between the front and rear walls of the bowl, keeping the scoop warm while it does its chilling duty. □

Songs of Silence

#1,776,584: 1930

Aspiring singers may choose to forestall complaints from their neighbors by using a muffling device patented by Stephen G. Gerlach, Jr. A tubular case with a wide mouth designed to fit over the singer's lower face, the muffler contains a series of baffles "whereby the vocal sounds produced by a person in the act of practicing singing may be effectually subdued, the sounds passing into the case and being effectually broken up . . . so that but little sound will be perceptible." □

Pot Boiler

A cook could stand well away from the stove and still stir the contents of a stovetop cooking pot with the help of a device patented by Abraham Caufman of Kansas. A horizontal crossbar grips the rim of the pot and supports a vertical shaft that thrusts down into the cooking vessel. The stirring element is linked through a pair of differential gears to a horizontal handle, which the cook turns to produce the circular stirring motion of the shaft in the pot. □

#268,185: 1882

Waterfingers

Squirting games played with a water pistol can also be played with the water glove patented by Eddie A. Sirhan of California. By pressing a button, the user shoots a thin, pulsating stream of water from a pinhole in one of the fingertips. A tube connects the hole to a reservoir pack and battery-operated pump clipped to the operator's belt. Unlike a water pistol, the water glove is not made of hard plastic and thus cannot cause injuries, "even in the heat of competition." □

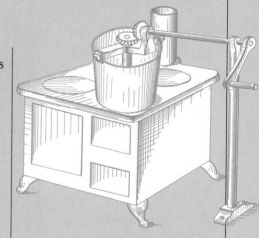

#4,903,864: 1990

BEYOND INGENUITY

Perhaps the hardest idea for the creative mind to grasp is the notion of its own boundaries. For the ingenious inventor, impossibility is a hostile and alien concept. Even so, some things do indeed appear to be impossible: time travel, for instance; or unaided human flight; or the transmuting of ordinary metals into great quantities of gold; or the making of machines that run eternally, constantly replenishing their own energy to perform their never-ending work. All known natural laws conspire against such ambitious dreams, but the dreams persist. The inventive mind cannot accept limitations, cannot believe that some achievements lie beyond human ingenuity.

And so the quest goes on, and seekers still traverse the uncharted land of wondrous mirages and elusive visions, hoping somehow to breach the barriers of physical laws and achieve the unachievable.

Gold Rush

More than 2,000 years ago, the idea arose among the Greeks of Alexandria that common metals could be transmuted into precious gold. Called alchemy, this experimental concept spread to the Arab world and then to western Europe, where it became the Middle Ages' version of chemistry.

Perhaps inspired by fairly simple chemical transformations they saw in metallurgists' workshops, hopeful experimenters toiled to make such base metals as lead into the noble one of gold, using some transforming elixir. A number of frauds claimed success, but, in fact, the alchemists' efforts invariably fizzled. Even the brilliant seventeenth-century English physicist Isaac Newton, who believed in the tenets of alchemy, tried his hand and failed.

Although neither Isaac Newton nor the earliest alchemists in Egypt could have known it, the transmutation of elements cannot be accomplished merely by a chemical reaction. Rather, changes must occur down in the very core of individual atoms, the basic constituents of matter.

In the nineteenth century, scientists found that radioactive materials like uranium were unstable; that is, their atomic composition was such that they would break down, or decay, into more-stable elements such as lead. From this discovery, the idea took hold that, if one could just tamper with the structure of atoms, one element could change into another—into gold, perhaps.

But not until 1937 did anyone detect even a transmuted trace of

In this seventeenth-century painting by Thomas Wyck, an alchemist pores over arcane tomes in a laboratory cluttered with tools of the trade, including such distillation vessels as the alembic below.

the precious metal. Then, a minute quantity of gold was created in an atom smasher when University of California physicists blasted platinum with a stream of subatomic particles called neutrons. The result was an unstable form of platinum that soon decayed, turning into a radioactive form of gold. But this first transmuted gold was itself unstable and decayed in a matter of days.

Since then, physicists have learned how to use the powerful atomic accelerators available today to produce gold in its stable form. But the amount yielded by each experiment in the multimillion-dollar accelerators is worth less than a billionth of a cent. Thus, man-made gold is even rarer and costlier than the natural stuff, and, for all practical purposes, the ancient dream of the alchemists still goes unfulfilled. □

As alchemists searched for a way to turn base metals into gold, they also tried to invent a universal solvent, perhaps as a way of cleaning their transmuted treasure. Such a solvent would be able to dissolve all matter, much as water dissolves salt. But the notion of a universal solvent raises a thought-provoking paradox: In what kind of container could one keep a substance capable of dissolving everything? Neither the alchemists nor their scientific successors have ever answered the question.

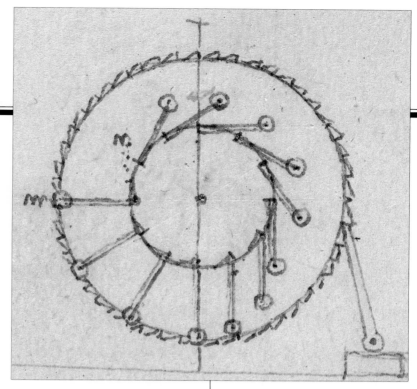

Endless Motion

While skeptical of perpetual motion, Leonardo da Vinci drew unbalanced wheels intended to spin forever.

As long ago as the sixteenth century, the idea of perpetual motion was ridiculed. The great Leonardo da Vinci said that those seeking to build machines that would run forever were credulous fools who might just as well join the alchemists in their quest to convert worthless metals into gold. Leonardo's opinion was widely shared, both then and now.

Even so, scientists and inventors of every era have been tempted by the prospect of getting more out of machinery than they put in. Countless ideas have made their way past the drawing board, some of them ingenious indeed. But all share the same fatal flaw: The concept of endless, unreplenished energy goes against basic physics.

Machines designed to keep going eternally run up against the first law of thermodynamics, which holds that energy cannot be created or destroyed. Since, by definition, the total energy in a perpetual-motion device cannot change, and since friction is inevi-

table, some of the budgeted energy is transformed into heat and lost to the surroundings, ultimately forcing the machine to a halt.

Noting this barrier, inventive perpetualists have attempted to divert this lost energy back into the machine to keep things going. But here, the second law of thermodynamics intervenes: Like water running downhill, heat only flows from hot to cold. The "steeper" the temperature difference, the greater the flow. But as the cold side inevitably warms up, the flow of energy diminishes; when temperatures are equal, it stops, and so does the machine it powers.

In spite of these fundamental barriers to perpetual motion, the idea has attracted its share of inventors. Even Leonardo, who obviously knew better, was not wholly immune: His private notebooks contain his own detailed sketches of no fewer than six perpetual-motion machines. □

Mechanical Mirages

Through the centuries, designs for perpetual-motion machines have featured an assortment of wheels, cogs, screws, pulleys, and pendulums, all propelled by some readily available source of energy, such as water or gravity. While the devices stretched scientific principles beyond their limits, they were often conceived so cleverly and built so skillfully that even skeptics could be convinced that the designers had accomplished the impossible.

Because the wheel is itself perpetual in the sense that it is a never-ending circle, it was a frequent starting point for aspiring perpetualists. Water clocks—timepieces controlled by a descending flow of water—and wheels driven by water probably inspired the earliest notions of endless motion. The first written record of the idea may be a fifth-century-AD Sanskrit manuscript describing a self-turning wheel run by mercury sloshing back and forth inside tubes around its rim. This is also the earliest written evidence of one of the most popular and persistent forms of perpetual-motion designs: the overbalanced wheel. In this device, shifting weights keep one side of the wheel always heavier than the other, with gravity pulling down the heavy side. But no matter how finely the device is adjusted, the two sides of the imbalanced wheel eventually cancel each other out. Balance is achieved, and the mechanism stops cold.

Medieval "motionists" turned their attention to the uses of falling water, hoping to harness and recycle it to drive a perpetually functioning machine. This hope was best represented by the Archimedean screw—an invention for pumping water uphill, named for the third-century-BC mathematician Archimedes. In one version, water cascades over a waterwheel to turn a millstone and, at the base of the cascade, to rotate one end of a long, coiled pipe: the Archimedean screw. As the pipe turns, threads scoop up water and carry it to the head of the cascade; it once more flows down, turning the stone and rotating the screw.

In theory, the concept is foolproof: The screw lifts water uphill; the water then flows down steps and gains force to drive a wheel that, in turn, rotates the screw. But in practice the cascade of water packs too little power to turn a screw large enough to carry sufficient water to keep the mechanism running. Still, the Archimedean screw was a compelling design, and when models failed, it was common for the chagrined inventors to blame unskilled carpenters.

The failure of such relatively simple contrivances compelled inventors to seek other, more sophisticated means of running their perpetual-motion machines. Many turned to magnets as a potential source of power. In 1570, an Italian Jesuit, Johannes Taisnierus, sketched the earliest recorded design of its type. His machine used a magnet placed at the upper end of a ramp. The magnet would pull an iron ball up the slope until it fell through a hole near the top, then rolled back to its starting point, where the cycle resumed. Despite many variations on the plan, the machine had no hope of working, for a magnet strong enough to drag the ball up a steep slope would be too powerful to let the ball drop through the hole.

In the 1700s and 1800s, enterprising inventors tried to modulate the energy sources themselves. They purported to turn magnetism or gravity on and off to create imbalances that would turn a wheel. Some claims were made for "magnetic attraction interceptors" and "gravity-interrupters"—but all were fraudulent. Such schemes gave way to designs using floats and weights submerged in liquids, or running on energy released by the compression and expansion of gas. The budding science of electromagnetism also gained attention from perpetual-motion devotees.

Despite the nineteenth-century discovery of physical laws that demonstrated that perpetual motion was impossible, many inventors were not to be deterred. A perpetual-motion mania swept through Europe and America. More than 500 patents for perpetual-motion machines were issued in England between 1855 and 1903. But the days of perpetual-motion devices were numbered.

To patent one in the United States today is not easy. Since 1911, the Patent Office has required, only for perpetual-motion patents, something above and beyond the usual drawings: a working model. None has appeared. □

126

Perpetual Devotion

Since 1979, a machine invented in a Mississippi garage has been the focus of bitter litigation, dividing scientists and government patent agents into armed camps of believers and infidels—and showing that the road to endless energy may lead only to perpetual commotion.

On March 22, 1979, inventor Joseph Newman of Lucedale, Mississippi, submitted a patent application to the U.S. Patent and Trademark Office for a machine he called a "revolutionary energy invention." The device was based on his hypothesis that matter is actually a compressed form of electromagnetic energy. Using relatively small amounts of electricity to generate a large electromagnetic field in a coil, the machine, according to Newman, puts out more energy than it receives from its battery power source. Patent officials were not convinced. Newman was denied a patent on the grounds that his device "smacks of a perpetual motion machine."

Following the decision, Newman filed suit against the Patent Office. A District of Columbia federal district court ordered that a thorough study of the invention be conducted by the National Bureau of Standards, now the National Institute of Standards and Technology. After a series of studies, the agency concluded that "at all conditions tested, the input power exceeded the output power. That is, the device did not deliver more energy than it used." After reviewing the study, the court concluded the motor was not patentable and ruled against Newman.

But the tenacious inventor disagreed with the institute's testing procedure and appealed to a higher court. In July 1989, a federal appeals court upheld the previous ruling, saying it found no error in the lower court's analysis.

Newman's argument that his machine had been improperly tested was countered by the appellate court's reply that the inventor "had a copy of the test before testing began" and that "Mr. Newman had a duty to raise objections, before or during testing, to any defects in the test protocol."

Many scientists support the government findings and dismiss the energy machine as just another in the centuries-old lineup of inventions that promise to produce more energy than they take in. But Newman still stands by his machine. He denies it was intended to be a perpetual-motion machine, although he believes that it could help solve the world's energy problems. The inventor claims that he has obtained seven foreign patents, as well as nearly a million dollars in financial backing for his device. He has also received support from some reputable scientists.

Following the appellate court's decision, Newman petitioned the U.S. Supreme Court to review his case. While waiting for its decision, he was ordered by the district court to pay more than $100,000 to the Patent Office for expenses incurred by the government in testing his device. In April 1990, Newman filed for bankruptcy. Barely three weeks later, the U.S. Supreme Court denied his request for a formal review. Despite Newman's unshaken faith in his invention, thus far it has propelled him mainly toward financial ruin. □

Inventor Joseph Newman adjusts a controversial magnetic device that he believes produces more energy than is required to run it.

Big Bird

Among the most common human dreams are dreams of flying—of soaring, free and unaided, the way birds do. But this happy vision will never be a waking reality. Evolution simply did not endow the human body with the proper aerodynamic gear. In order to fly without aircraft, people would have to undergo massive structural alterations to accommodate their comparatively great weight.

Had humanity achieved a winged subspecies, it might have resembled bats or large flying lizards called pterosaurs, long since extinct. Instead of hands, the arms of a flying human might have had greatly extended fingers, covered with a membrane of skin to serve as wings. Enormous muscles would have evolved to flap such huge pinions—muscles with many times the strength and endurance of any existing human muscles. The legs, too, would have become more powerful, to provide a faster takeoff run. Bone density and brain size would also probably have changed—bones and brain both becoming lighter—to accommodate the special requirements of an aerial life.

For years, most scientists believed that weight was the threshold barrier to human flight. The upper limit for sustained, wing-powered flight, they thought, was about forty pounds—the weight of a large goose or turkey. Beyond that limit, it seemed, natural fliers had to lift their greater weight with vast wings designed for soaring, not steady flapping.

In 1980, however, paleontologists made an aeronautically disquieting discovery in the Argentine pampas. Embedded in eight-million-year-old siltstone were the fossil remains of *Argentavis magnificens*. Before its extinction, the huge bird was borne aloft on twenty-three-foot feathered wings—wings that allowed both flapping and soaring. And this creature was no lightweight. Its remains suggested that it weighed about 200 pounds, the weight of a good-size human.

In any event, *Argentavis magnificens* was a bird. The evolutionary scheme produced few winged mammals, and, obviously, no winged humans. To satisfy its age-old longing for flight, humanity followed the path of mechanical, not evolutionary, invention. □

The Impossible Achieved

Over the past thousand years, would-be aviators have strapped themselves to crudely constructed wings and leaped from castle walls, towers, and cliffs. Some plunged to their deaths; others, more fortunate, merely suffered broken bones and shattered dreams.

Neither bird imitators nor the scientists of their day realized that human muscles are too weak to sustain a wing beat and that clumsy mechanical flapping is insufficient to propel a person into the air. Even fifteenth-century scientific genius Leonardo da Vinci—who devoted considerable amounts of time and study to the matter of human flight—erroneously believed that the artificial wings of a flying machine would have to flap.

For nearly 500 years, sustained, human-powered flight remained an enticing challenge, and even in modern times some adventurous souls refused to abandon the idea. In 1959, British industrialist Henry Kremer offered a £5,000 prize for the first human-powered aircraft to fly nonstop around a prescribed course. Determined by England's Royal Aeronautical Society, the course required competitors to fly a figure eight around two pylons spaced half a mile apart, plus cross over the start and finish lines at an altitude of at least ten feet. Many entrants from Britain, Germany, Austria, and Japan failed in their attempts, and by 1973, the Kremer prize was raised to £50,000 (about $123,500 then).

On August 23, 1977, 135-pound American bicyclist Bryan Allen finally conquered the course, piloting a craft that weighed only half as much as he did. Feverishly pedaling the *Gossamer Condor*—a frail, ungainly airplane with a ninety-six-foot wingspan—Allen wafted to victory at an airstrip in Shafter, California. The designer of the ultralightweight plane was aeronautical engineer and international soaring champion Paul Mac-Ready. He collected the prize and made aviation history with his skillfully assembled craft built mostly from thin, transparent plastic; corrugated cardboard; alumi-

num tubing; and piano wire. Two bicycle-type pedals in front of the pilot's seat connected to a chain-driven propeller at the rear of the plane. MacReady dubbed the *Condor* a "quick sloppy beast" constructed with "just the right amount of flimsy."

Nearly three years later, a second MacReady-designed aircraft captured a second Kremer prize: £100,000 promised to anyone who flew a human-powered airplane across the English Channel. Again, twenty-six-year-old Allen provided the power. He pedaled the *Gossamer Albatross* for an agonizing two hours and forty-nine minutes to cover the 22.5 miles from the southeast coast of England to Cap Gris Nez, France. Landing on the beach after an ordeal in turbulent air and headwinds, Allen commented, "What audacity to challenge the elements in such a machine."

In 1988, a championship cyclist and a design team from the Massachusetts Institute of Technology (MIT) attempted to duplicate a mythical human-powered flight: that of Daedalus, the legendary Greek architect who supposedly flew from Crete to the Aegean island of Santorin on wings of wax and feathers. (According to myth, Icarus, his son, flew too close to the sun, which melted the wax that held his wings together. Icarus fell to his death in the sea.) On April 23, the forty-member MIT team watched their three-year, one-million-dollar project soar to success as the 68.5-pound *Daedalus 88* retraced the ancient journey on

a 112-foot gossamer wing.

Pilot Kanellos Kanellopoulos, a fourteen-time Greek cycling champion, was well prepared for the strenuous 72-mile pedal. His preflight diet consisted of nearly 7,000 low-fat, high-carbohydrate calories. And, his strict seven-month training regimen included bicycling more than 10,000 miles—sometimes 100 miles a day, mostly uphill. He was so aerobically fit, his body could process oxygen twice as well as that of the average person.

Daedalus 88 weighed so little because it was made mostly of a lightweight material called graphite epoxy, which can withstand more stress than aluminum and similar lightweight materials.

Kanellopoulos flew the *Daedalus 88* for a record three hours and fifty-four minutes. Flight conditions were perfect, except for a troublesome headwind encountered as the plane prepared to land. Just thirty feet from shore, the tail boom ripped apart, and the craft splashed down gently; the pilot dove through the thin plastic wing covering to safety in the water.

Although such flights demonstrated that human-powered flight is possible, they also showed that it was not for everyone. Not even the most advanced aircraft design can overcome the inevitable exhaustion of its power source: the muscles in the pilot's body. Human muscles, unlike those of birds, quickly reach their limits. □

Early attempts at human-powered flight *(top)* were aerodynamically doomed to failure. But in 1977, Bryan Allen pedaled the lightweight *Gossamer Condor* over a one-mile course and, nearly three years later, crossed the English Channel in the *Gossamer Albatross (center)*. In 1988, Kanellos Kanellopoulos flew the pedal-driven *Daedalus 88 (bottom)* more than three times farther: seventy-two miles across the Aegean.

The River of Time

Time seems to unfold in a seamless continuum in which the past flows into the present, and the present blends imperceptibly into the future. This seeming continuity has suggested to generations of inventors that there must be a way of moving from one point in time to another. It is more than wishful thinking: Despite daunting technical problems, many scientists believe that human time travel is at least theoretically possible.

In 1905, Albert Einstein hypothesized that time is not constant everywhere in the universe: The faster something—or someone—travels, the more the traveler's time slows down, at least from the perspective of an outside observer. For example, if an identical twin zips through space at a speed approaching that of light (about 186,000 miles per second), he will be younger than his earthbound brother when he returns. The faster the twin travels and the longer his journey, the farther into the future he will find himself upon his return to earth, although he will have aged relatively less. Such travelers are, in effect, moved into the future by the distortions of their time.

But no space vehicle now flying or envisioned will even begin to approach the speed of light, and the speed achieved by existing spacecraft causes time distortions so small that they can barely be measured. For example, an astronaut who orbits the earth once ages only one-billionth of a second less than his ground-control crew. Still, technical obstacles aside, hurtling into the future, however improbable, is not beyond the realm of possibility.

Travel to the past, however, is very likely impossible. The future, in Einstein's view, is in some respects accessible. But the past ceases to exist. Still, if it were there to visit—if time did indeed flow like a river—journeys to the past offer mind-boggling paradoxes of causality, a scientific principle that says everything that happens has a cause. Traveling backward in time could alter past events and thus change future ones in ways that are not easily comprehended. The example that scientists usually offer for this theoretical phenomenon is called the grandfather paradox: If one travels into the past and kills one's grandfather before he can sire children, the grandfather's descendants, including the time traveler, are erased. But, if erased, how did the traveler exist in the first place to go back to kill his grandfather? Such hazards and paradoxes have stimulated less science than fiction, which remains the only province where humans travel easily from era to era. □

Actor Rod Taylor sits at the helm of *The Time Machine* in the 1960 film version of H. G. Wells's classic tale.

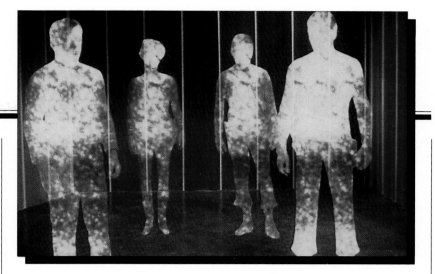

Ties that Blind

All so-called solid matter is mostly space, or, as one scientist put it, "specks of electricity in an enormous void." The tiny universe inside the atoms and molecules of everything that appears to be solid has empty reaches as proportionately vast as the distances between stars. With so much apparently empty space between the "specks," it would seem feasible to invent a way to pass two solid objects— inert or alive—through each other without a scrape. But in fact, it is not possible.

The space inside both the molecules and the atoms that compose them is not as empty as it seems. All solids depend on a precise molecular structure—an internal architecture—that is held together by electricity and other unseen forces. Space, however empty, is an essential part of the architecture. Passing one solid object through another would rip this invisible structure apart, causing such molecular chaos that neither object would survive the encounter in a recognizable form. □

Robert Lansing makes the physically impossible look easy as he walks through walls in 1959's *4D Man*.

Lear Net

In the mid-1950s, the inventor of the fast, compact Lear Jet predicted that his plane would soon be outpaced by a machine with neither wings nor wheels, one that never left the ground. No larger than a telephone booth, the device envisioned by William P. Lear, Sr., would disintegrate passengers into "electronic vibrations" and transport them to their destinations within a few seconds, at the mere push of a button.

Lear's idea of transmitting dissociated people and objects from place to place may very well be an impossible invention. Despite the familiar "Beam me up, Scotty!" of television's *Star Trek (above)*, breaking the body into electronic particles—or atomic or molecular particles, for that matter—and reassembling them somewhere else may ask too much of any life form, especially one as large and complex as a human being. More likely, the kind of teleportation network described by Lear would deal in replications rather than in the genuine article.

Already, sophisticated electronics permits facsimile images to be sent around the world in seconds. The original images themselves do not actually travel from one place to another; instead, they are replicated at the destination point from descriptive digital information sent via telephone. Perhaps, some scientists believe, a more advanced system would be able to send enough information to replicate solid objects—and, perhaps, living beings. For example, a device might scan its subject, atom by atom, to describe every billionth of a cubic inch, then send that information to the receiving end. There, a warehouse of sorts would store the atomic ingredients needed to reconstruct the three-dimensional object described by incoming electronic impulses.

Practically speaking, however, such replication may only be feasible for very simple objects. Duplicating something as complicated as a human being would present tremendous stumbling blocks. True, the warehouse would only need to stock a few dollars' worth of raw materials to replicate a human body. But there would be some delay at the transmitting end. If the transmitter scanned a body at the same rate that a modern facsimile machine scans images, collecting the necessary atom-by-atom data could take thousands of centuries. And no one knows how such a device could transmit detailed descriptions of a person's thoughts, emotions, and individual eccentricities. □

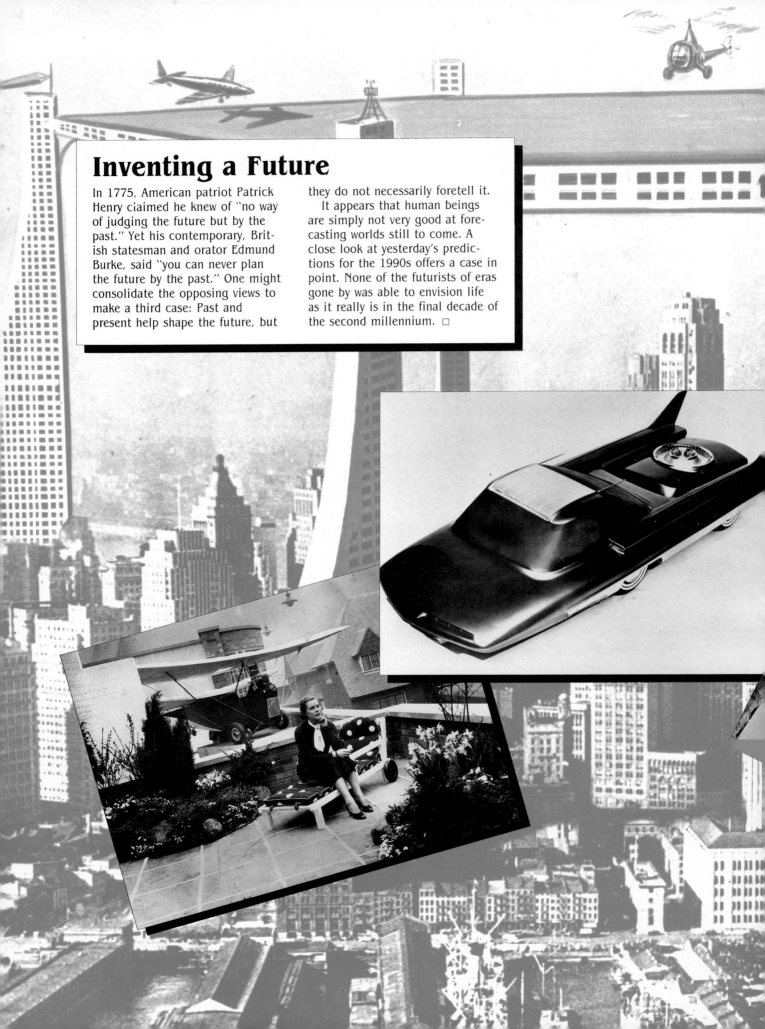

Inventing a Future

In 1775, American patriot Patrick Henry claimed he knew of "no way of judging the future but by the past." Yet his contemporary, British statesman and orator Edmund Burke, said "you can never plan the future by the past." One might consolidate the opposing views to make a third case: Past and present help shape the future, but they do not necessarily foretell it.

It appears that human beings are simply not very good at forecasting worlds still to come. A close look at yesterday's predictions for the 1990s offers a case in point. None of the futurists of eras gone by was able to envision life as it really is in the final decade of the second millennium. □

Earlier in the twentieth century, forecasts for its final decade predicted an aircraft in every garage (or on every rooftop) and widespread uses of atomic power, including reactor-powered cars. High-speed motorways with guide tracks would end congestion and make highway travel accident free. At home, lovable mechanical servants would cook, clean, and baby-sit, while cities such as the one depicted in the background would thrive in giant, weather-controlled incubators whose spacious roofs could serve as airstrips.

Beyond 2000

Given the failure of futurists past to predict the shape of life in the 1990s, how well will today's futurists fare in portraying a third millennium? After assessing a number of political and social trends, modern prophets refine their view of the future on the basis of computer simulations, the views of leaders in technology, and other forecasting clues. They also employ a predictive method called backcasting, in which numerous future scenarios are proposed, then experts work backward to determine what events would have to occur for each possibility to be realized. According to these experts, the most likely future is the one whose patterns most closely resemble those that are already developing today. Whether the futurists of today will come closer to the mark than their earlier counterparts remains to be seen. □

Present-day futurists predict a third millennium vastly modified by technologies just surfacing today. The computerized dashboard-map display shown at far left, for example, may be the precursor of a fully computerized, high-volume system of traffic control. Domed lunar colonies *(center)* are foreseen as bases for mining and space industries, the harsh environment softened through artificial photosynthesis and a partial greening of the moon. Biotechnologies may permit scientists to re-create extinct animals such as the *Plateosaurus* below, for study in closed island habitats. Cities of the 2000s, some believe, will accommodate a vastly increased global population with skyscrapers that, like the thousand-story structures pictured here, truly reach the sky.

ACKNOWLEDGMENTS

The editors wish to thank these individuals and institutions for their valuable assistance in the preparation of this volume:

Paul-Jean Bousquet, Concours Lépine, Paris; Kenneth E. Campbell, Natural History Museum of Los Angeles County, Los Angeles; Paul Ceruzzi, National Air and Space Museum, Washington, D.C.; Umberto Colomo, ENEA, Rome; Beverly Cutten, Cliff Petersen Patent Model Collection, Garrison, New York; John Dale, Esperanto Society of Washington, D.C.; Nancy Dempsey, Xerox Corporation, Rochester, New York; Diane Dickey, Kellogg Company, Battle Creek, Michigan; André Dubisson, Mairie de Sées, Sées, France; Robert Flamant, Concours Lépine, Paris; Danielle Frizzi, Gillette Company, Boston, Massachusetts; David Gaines, Esperanto Society of Washington, D.C.; J. Morgan Green, United States Patent Model Foundation, Alexandria, Virginia; Tracey Guerra, Chesebrough-Pond's Inc., Greenwich, Connecticut; Matthias Heister, Deutsche Aktionsgemeinschaft Bildung-Erfindung-Innovation, Bonn; Barbara Horner, Talon Inc., Meadville, Pennsylvania; Robert Kwalwasser, Renfrew, Pennsylvania; J. A. Lelorrain, Maison Alice Cadolle, Paris; Rita Levy, C.N.R., Rome; Jacquelyn B. Love, Hoover Company, North Canton, Ohio; Francesca Marotti, Rome; Oscar Mastin, Public Affairs Office, the Patent and Trademark Office, Arlington, Virginia; Nancy J. Metz, United States Patent Model Foundation, Alexandria, Virginia; William A. Meyers, Southern California Edison Company, Rosemead; Ann Milbrooke, United Technologies, East Hartford, Connecticut; Philip F. Mooney, Coca-Cola Company, Atlanta, Georgia; Steve Novak, Cliff Petersen Patent Model Collection, Garrison, New York; Andreas Paetzold, Deutsches Patentamt, Munich; Cliff Petersen, Phoenix, Arizona; Franca Principe, Istituto e Museo di Storia della Scienza, Florence; Carlo Rusconi, Società Italiana Brevetti, Rome; Pierluigi Sani, ENEA, Rome; Ed Sobey, National Inventors Hall of Fame and the National Invention Center, Akron, Ohio; Barbara E. Sorenson, National Museum of Roller Skating, Lincoln, Nebraska; Sergio Stingo, Milan; Giorgio Strini, Società Italiana Brevetti, Rome; Michele Szynal, Gillette Company, Boston, Massachusetts; Richard Tweddell, Cincinnati, Ohio; Mona Verhelst, Conté, Nanterre, Hauts-de-Seine, France; Elizabeth Walter, General Motors Engineering and Management Institute, Flint, Michigan.

PICTURE CREDITS

The sources for the pictures are listed below. Credits from left to right are separated by semicolons, from top to bottom by dashes.

Cover: Inset, Charles O'Rear/Westlight, Los Angeles, background, Comstock, New York. **3:** Charles O'Rear/Westlight, Los Angeles. **7:** Inset, Mander and Mitchenson Theatre Collection, London, background, M. Angelo/Westlight, Los Angeles. **8, 9:** Scala, Florence, courtesy Biblioteca Reale, Turin (2); Scala, Florence, courtesy Institut de France, Paris; Scala, Florence, courtesy Museo Vinciano, Venici. **10:** From *The Pneumatics of Hero of Alexandria*, Macdonald & Company, London, American Elsevier Company, New York, 1971. **11:** Philadelphia Museum of Art, Mr. and Mrs. Wharton Sinkler Collection, Philadelphia—courtesy the Franklin Institute Science Museum, Philadelphia. **12:** Royal Artillery Institution, London; Smithsonian Institution 32825-T. **13:** Department of Rare Books & Collections, University of Michigan Library, Ann Arbor. **14:** Culver Pictures Inc., New York. **15:** Chicago Historical Society, Chicago—courtesy Silvio A. Bedini. **16:** Culver Pictures Inc., New York—UPI/Bettmann Archive, New York. **17:** Courtesy National Park Service, Ford's Theatre, Washington, D.C./photograph by Edward Owen. **18:** Library of Congress USZ62-14760—Smithsonian Institution 47797-A. **19:** Bruce Zake, courtesy the Goodyear Hall of Fame, Akron, Ohio, © 1990; Library of Congress USZ62-7162. **20:** Library of Congress USZ62-100649—Smithsonian Institution 649-L. **21:** Library of Congress. **22:** Courtesy the New York Historical Society, New York—Metropolitan Museum of Art, New York, gift of I. N. Phelps Stokes, Edward S. Hawes, Alice Mary Hawes, Marion Augusta Hawes, 1937. **23:** Smithsonian Institution 86-6162. **24:** Courtesy Burndy Library, Norwalk, Connecticut; Richard Pasley © 1987. **25:** Courtesy Hagley Museum and Library, Wilmington, Delaware—UPI/Bettmann Archive, New York. **26:** Courtesy AT&T Archives, Warren, New Jersey. **27:** Smithsonian Institution 86-6161. **28:** Mander and Mitchenson Theatre Collection, London. **29:** Courtesy Levi Strauss & Co., San Francisco. **30, 31:** Smithsonian Institution 90-8982; Burndy Library, Norwalk, Connecticut. **32:** AP/Wide World Photos, New York. **33:** Courtesy Kliegl Brothers, Syosset, New York. **34:** B. Rheims/Sygma, New York. **35:** Science Museum, London. **37:** UPI/Bettmann Archive, New York—Missouri Historical Society, St. Louis. **38:** Süddeutscher Verlag Bilderdienst, Munich. **39:** GMI Alumni Foundations Collection of Industrial History, Flint, Michigan. **40:** Western Reserve Historical Society, Cleveland; Moorland-Springarn Research Center, Howard University, Washington, D.C. **41:** Library of Congress USZ62-6166A. **42:** From *Rube Goldberg vs. the Machine Age*, by Clark Kinnaird, Hastings House, New York, 1968—Culver Pictures Inc., New York. **43:** Movie Star News, New York. **44:** Larry Sherer/*Time* magazine cover. **45:** Courtesy Jacuzzi Archives. **46:** Courtesy Chris Beetles Ltd., St. James's, London, sole agent of Rowland and Mary Emett. **47:** Inset, Polaroid Corporate Archives, Cambridge, Massachusetts, background, Westlight, Los Angeles. **48:** The Granger Collection, New York. **49:** George S. Bolster Collection, Historical Society of Saratoga Springs, New York. **50:** Ann Ronan Picture Library, Taunton, Sussex—ICI Specialities, Historical Archives, Blackley, England. **51:** Culver Pictures Inc., New York; courtesy Procter & Gamble Company, Cincinnati. **52:** Roger-Viollet, Paris. **53:** The Granger Collection, New York; Culver Pictures Inc., New York. **54:** Courtesy Scott Paper Company, Philadelphia. **55:** UPI/Bettmann Archive, New York (2); the Granger Collection, New York. **56:** Courtesy the Masonite Corporation, Building Products Group, Chicago. **58, 59:** Fil Hunter. **60:** Art by Time-Life Books—Nationalgalerie der Staatlichen Museen Preussischer Kulturbesitz, Berlin. **61:** National Cash Register, Dayton, Ohio. **62:** Larry Sherer, courtesy the Mt. Vernon Museum of Incandescent Lighting, Baltimore. **63:** Outboard Marine Corporation, Waukegan, Illinois. **64:** Library of Congress—courtesy Hagley Museum and Library, Wilmington, Delaware. **65:** UPI/Bettmann Archive, New York. **66:** Johnson & Johnson, New Brunswick, New Jersey; Evan Sheppard. **67:** National Inventors Hall of Fame, Akron, Ohio. **68, 69:** Polaroid Corporate Archives, Cambridge, Massachusetts. **70:** Copied by Larry Sherer, from *The Cart That Changed the World: The Career of Sylvan N. Goldman*, by Terry P. Wilson, University of Oklahoma Press, Norman, 1978—Smithsonian Institution. **71:** Roy Stevens. **72:** Yves Debraine, Lausanne. **73:** Courtesy Gihon Foundation, by permission of Michael Nesmith, Dallas. **74:** Wally Nelson, *Dayton Daily News*, Dayton, Ohio. **75:** Courtesy

BIBLIOGRAPHY

Books

Aaseng, Nathan:
    Better Mousetraps: Product Improvements That Led to Success. Minneapolis: Lerner Publications, 1990.
    The Inventors: Nobel Prizes in Chemistry, Physics, and Medicine. Minneapolis: Lerner Publications, 1988.
Adams, Russell B., Jr. *King C. Gillette: The Man and His Wonderful Shaving Device.* Boston: Little, Brown, 1978.
Allister, Ray. *Friese-Greene: Close-Up of an Inventor.* London: Marsland Publications, 1948.
American Enterprise: Nineteenth-Century Patent Models. New York: Cooper-Hewitt Museum, 1984.
Ames, J. S. (Ed.). *Memoirs by Joseph Henry* (Vol. 1 of *The Discovery of Induced Electric Currents*). New York: American Book Co., 1900.
Andrews, Edward Deming:
    The Community Industries of the Shakers. Philadelphia: Porcupine Press, 1972.

The People Called Shakers. New York: Dover, 1963.
The Annual Obituary 1986. Chicago: St. James Press, 1989.
Barker, Preston Wallace. *Charles Goodyear: Connecticut Yankee and Rubber Pioneer.* Boston: Godfrey L. Cabot, 1940.
Bathe, Greville. *Three Essays: A Dissertation on the Genesis of Mechanical Transport in America Before 1800.* St. Augustine, Fla.: Historical Society of Pennsylvania, 1960.
Bathe, Greville, and Dorothy Bathe. *Oliver Evans: A Chronicle of Early American Engineering.* Philadelphia: Historical Society of Pennsylvania, 1935.
Bedini, Silvio A. *Thomas Jefferson: Statesman of Science.* London: Collier Macmillan, 1990.
Bell, Robert Charles. *Board and Table Games from Many Civilizations.* London: Oxford University Press, 1960.
Bergengren, Erik. *Alfred Nobel: The Man and His Work.* Translated by Alan Blair. London: Thomas Nelson & Sons, 1962.

Bowen, Catherine Drinker. *The Most Dangerous Man in America: Scenes from the Life of Benjamin Franklin.* Boston: Little, Brown, 1974.
Boyd, Thomas Alvin. *Professional Amateur: The Biography of Charles Franklin Kettering.* New York: E. P. Dutton, 1957.
Brown, Kenneth A. *Inventors at Work.* Tell City, Ind.: Tempus, 1988.
Bruce, Robert V. *Bell: Alexander Graham Bell and the Conquest of Solitude.* Boston: Little, Brown, 1973.
Brumbaugh, Robert S. *Ancient Greek Gadgets and Machines.* New York: Thomas Y. Crowell, 1975.
Burke, James. *Connections.* Boston: Little, Brown, 1978.
Caney, Steven. *Steven Caney's Invention Book.* New York: Workman, 1985.
Chanan, Michael. *The Dream That Kicks: The Prehistory and Early Years of Cinema in Britain.* London: Routledge & Kegan Paul, 1980.
Cheney, Margaret. *Tesla: Man Out of Time.* New

York: Dell, 1981.

Cipolla, Carlo M., and Derek Birdsall. *The Technology of Man*. New York: Holt, Rinehart & Winston, 1979.

Clarke, Arthur C. *Profiles of the Future*. New York: Holt, Rinehart & Winston, 1984.

Clarke, Donald (Ed.). *The Encyclopedia of How It Works from Abacus to Zoom Lens*. New York: A & W, 1978.

Cooper, Margaret. *The Inventions of Leonardo da Vinci*. New York: Macmillan, 1965.

Corn, Joseph J. (Ed.). *Imagining Tomorrow: History, Technology, and the American Future*. Cambridge, Mass.: MIT Press, 1986.

Costain, Thomas B. *The Chord of Steel: The Story of the Invention of the Telephone*. Garden City, N.Y.: Doubleday, 1960.

Crawford, T. S. *A History of the Umbrella*. New York: Taplinger, 1970.

de Bono, Edward (Ed.). *Eureka! An Illustrated History of Inventions from the Wheel to the Computer*. New York: Holt, Rinehart & Winston, 1972.

de Camp, L. Sprague. *The Ancient Engineers*. Garden City, N.Y.: Doubleday, 1963.

The Development of Modern Science (Vol. 2 of *Moments of Discovery*). New York: Basic Books, 1958.

Eco, Umberto, and G. B. Zorzoli. *The Picture History of Inventions: From Plough to Polaris*. Translated by Anthony Lawrence. New York: Macmillan, 1963.

Edwards, William B. *Civil War Guns*. Secaucus, N.J.: Castle, 1982.

Ewing, Elizabeth. *Fashion in Underwear*. London: B. T. Batsford, 1971.

Fabell, Walter C. *Nature's Clues*. New York: Hastings House, 1964.

Feldman, Anthony, and Peter Ford. *Scientists & Inventors*. New York: Facts On File, 1979.

The 50 Great Pioneers of American Industry. By the Editors of News Front Year. Maplewood, N.J.: C. S. Hammond; New York: Year Inc., 1964.

Fitch, John. *The Original Steam-Boat*. Freeport, N.Y.: Books for Libraries Press, 1971 (reprint of 1788 edition).

Ford, Barbara. *The Elevator*. New York: Walker, 1982.

Fuller, Edmund. *Tinkers and Genius*. New York: Hastings House, 1955.

Giedion, Siegfried. *Mechanization Takes Command: A Contribution to Anonymous History*. New York: W. W. Norton, 1948.

Gies, Joseph, and Frances Gies. *The Ingenious Yankees*. New York: Thomas Y. Crowell, 1976.

Gillispie, Charles Coulston (Ed.). *Dictionary of Scientific Biography* (Vols. 1, 5). New York: Charles Scribner's Sons, 1980.

Gleasner, Diana C. *Dynamite*. New York: Walker,

1982.

Green, Fitzhugh. *A Change in the Weather*. New York: W. W. Norton, 1977.

Groner, Alex, and the Editors of *American Heritage* and *Business Week*. *American Business & Industry*. Edited by Alvin M. Josephy, Jr. New York: American Heritage, 1972.

Grosser, Morton. *Diesel: The Man & the Engine*. New York: Atheneum, 1978.

Hawke, David Freeman. *Nuts and Bolts of the Past*. New York: Harper & Row, 1988.

Hendrickson, Robert. *The Dictionary of Eponyms*. New York: Dorset Press, 1972.

Heydenreich, Ludwig H., Bern Dibner, and Ladislao Reti. *Leonardo the Inventor*. New York: McGraw-Hill, 1980.

Heyn, Ernest V. *A Century of Wonders*. Garden City, N.Y.: Doubleday, 1972.

Heyn, Ernest V., et al. *Fire of Genius: Inventors of the Past Century*. Garden City, N.Y.: Anchor Press/Doubleday, 1976.

Hodges, Henry. *Technology in the Ancient World*. New York: Alfred A. Knopf, 1970.

Hooper, Meredith. *Everyday Inventions*. New York: Taplinger, 1972.

Hoover, Frank G. *Fabulous Dustpan: The Story of the Hoover*. Cleveland: World Publishing, 1955.

Horn, Maurice (Ed.). *The World Encyclopedia of Comics*. New York: Avon, 1976.

Hughes, Thomas Parke:
American Genesis. New York: Viking, 1989.
Elmer Sperry: Inventor and Engineer. Baltimore: Johns Hopkins Press, 1971.

The Innovators: How Today's Inventors Shape Your Life Tomorrow. By the staff of the *Wall Street Journal*. Princeton, N.J.: Dow Jones Books, 1968.

The Inventive Yankee. By the publishers of *Yankee* magazine. Dublin, N.H.: Yankee Books, 1989.

James, Edward T., Janet Wilson James, and Paul S. Boyer (Eds.). *Notable American Women 1607-1950* (Vol. 2). Cambridge, Mass.: Belknap Press of Harvard University Press, 1971.

Jewkes, John, David Sawers, and Richard Stillerman. *The Sources of Invention* (2d ed.). New York: W. W. Norton, 1969.

Johnston, Ben. *My Inventions: The Autobiography of Nikola Tesla*. Williston, Vt.: Hart Brothers, 1982.

Jones, Stacy V.:
Inventions Necessity Is Not the Mother of Patents Ridiculous and Sublime. New York: Quadrangle/New York Times Book Co., 1973.
The Patent Office. New York: Praeger, 1971.

Joseph, John. *Merlin: The Ingenious Mechanick*. London: Greater London Council, 1985.

Kaempffert, Waldemar (Ed.). *A Popular History*

of American Invention (Vol. 1). New York: Charles Scribner's Sons, 1924.

Klein, Aaron E., and Cynthia L. Klein. *The Better Mousetrap*. New York: Beaufort Books, 1982.

Larsen, Egon. *Men Who Changed the World: Stories of Invention and Discovery*. London: Phoenix House, 1952.

Lasson, Kenneth. *Mousetraps and Muffling Cups*. New York: Arbor House, 1986.

Leslie, Stuart W. *Boss Kettering*. New York: Columbia University Press, 1983.

Lifshey, Earl. *The Housewares Story*. Chicago: National Housewares Manufacturers Association, 1973.

Lindbergh, Charles Augustus. *Autobiography of Values*. New York: Harcourt Brace Jovanovich, 1978.

Madigan, Carol Orsag, and Ann Elwood. *Brainstorms & Thunderbolts*. New York: Macmillan, 1983.

Marzio, Peter C. *Rube Goldberg: His Life and His Work*. New York: Harper & Row, 1973.

Metal Fabrication by Risdon. Naugatuck, Conn.: Risdon, 1945.

Moolman, Valerie, and the Editors of Time-Life Books. *The Road to Kitty Hawk* (The Epic of Flight series). Alexandria, Va.: Time-Life Books, 1980.

Morrison, Philip, and Emily Morrison. *Charles Babbage and His Calculating Engines*. New York: Dover, 1961.

Moselem, Maboth. *Irascible Genius: The Life of Charles Babbage*. Chicago: H. Regnery, 1970.

Neal, Harry Edward. *From Spinning Wheel to Spacecraft*. New York: Julian Messner, 1964.

The New Illustrated Science and Invention Encyclopedia. Westport, Conn.: H. S. Stuttman, 1989.

Newman, Joseph Westley. *The Energy Machine of Joseph Newman* (6th ed.). Edited by Evan R. Soulé, Jr. New Orleans: J. W. Newman, 1990.

Ord-Hume, Arthur W. J. G. *Perpetual Motion: The History of an Obsession*. New York: St. Martin's Press, 1977.

The Origins of Science (Vol. 1 of *Moments of Discovery*). New York: Basic Books, 1959.

Panati, Charles. *Extraordinary Origins of Everyday Things*. New York: Harper & Row, 1987.

Petroski, Henry. *The Pencil*. New York: Alfred A. Knopf, 1990.

Phin, John. *The Seven Follies of Science*. New York: D. Van Nostrand, 1906.

Piggott, Stuart. *The Earliest Wheeled Transport: From the Atlantic Coast to the Caspian Sea*. New York: Thames & Hudson, 1983.

Pizer, Vernon. *Shortchanged by History: America's Neglected Innovators*. New York: G. P. Putnam's Sons, 1979.

Poole, Lynn, and Gray Poole. *Men Who Pio-*

neered Inventions. New York: Dodd, Mead, 1969.

Presence, Peter (Ed.). Encyclopedia of Inventions. Secaucus, N.J.: Chartwell Books, 1976.

Pressman, David. Patent It Yourself (2d ed.). Edited by Stephen Elias. Berkeley: Nolo Press, 1988.

Randolph, Blythe. Charles Lindbergh. New York: Franklin Watts, 1990.

Richards, Norman. Dreamers & Doers: Inventors Who Changed Our World. New York: Atheneum, 1984.

Richards, Steve. Invisibility: Mastering the Art of Vanishing. San Bernardino, Calif.: Borgo Press, 1986.

Ross, Walter S. The Last Hero: Charles A. Lindbergh. New York: Harper & Row, 1968.

Rothenberg, Gunther E. The Art of Warfare in the Age of Napoleon. Bloomington: Indiana University Press, 1978.

Rothschild, Joan (Ed.). Women, Technology and Innovation. Oxford: Pergamon Press, 1982.

Slappey, Sterling G. (Comp.). Pioneers of American Business. New York: Grosset & Dunlap, 1973.

Small Inventions That Make a Big Difference. Washington, D.C.: National Geographic Society, 1984.

The Smithsonian Book of Invention. New York: W. W. Norton, 1978.

Temple, Robert. The Genius of China. New York: Simon & Schuster, 1986.

Toppin, Edgar Allen. A Biographical History of Blacks in America Since 1528. New York: David McKay, 1971.

Traub, Morris (Ed.). Roller Skating: Through the Years. New York: William-Frederick Press, 1944.

Usher, Abbott Payson. A History of Mechanical Inventions (rev. ed.). New York: Dover, 1954.

Vare, Ethlie Ann, and Greg Ptacek. Mothers of Invention. New York: William Morrow, 1988.

Wallace, Irving, David Wallechinsky, and Amy Wallace. Significa. New York: E. P. Dutton, 1983.

Wallace, Robert, and the Editors of Time-Life Books. The World of Leonardo 1452-1519 (Time-Life Library of Art series). New York: Time Inc., 1966.

Wallechinsky, David, and Irving Wallace. The People's Almanac. Garden City, N.Y.: Doubleday, 1975.

Webb, W. J., and Robert W. Carrick. The Pictorial History of Outboard Motors. New York: Renaissance Editions, 1967.

Wensberg, Peter C. Land's Polaroid. Boston: Houghton Mifflin, 1987.

Wertkin, Gerard C. The Four Seasons of Shaker Life: An Intimate Portrait of the Community at Sabbathday Lake. New York: Simon & Schuster, 1986.

White, Anna, and Leila S. Taylor. Shakerism: Its Meaning and Message. Columbus, Ohio: Fred J. Heer, 1905.

Wilkie, F. B. The Great Inventions. Philadelphia: J. A. Ruth, 1883.

Williams, Trevor I. The History of Invention. New York: Facts On File, 1987.

Wilson, Terry P. The Cart That Changed the World (Oklahoma Trackmaker series). Norman: University of Oklahoma Press, 1978.

Woodcroft, Bennet (Ed. & Trans.). The Pneumatics of Hero of Alexandria. New York: American Elsevier, 1971.

Zinsser, Hans. Rats, Lice and History. Boston: Little, Brown, 1963.

Periodicals

Allen, Bryan. "Winged Victory of 'Gossamer Albatross.'" National Geographic, November 1979.

Anderson, John. "Who Really Invented the Video Game?" Creative Computing, October 1982.

Aronson, Robert B. "The Futile Quest for Perpetual Motion." Machine Design, March 11, 1982.

Bloom, Steve. "Video Games Interview: Ralph Baer." Video Games, February 1983.

Brown, Paul B. "Staying Power." Forbes, March 26, 1984.

Campbell, Kenneth E., and Leslie Marcus. "How Big Was It?: Determining the Size of Ancient Birds." Terra, Summer 1990.

"Chester F. Carlson: Inventor of Xerography." Photographic Science and Engineering, January-February 1963.

"Clarence Birdseye Is Dead at 69; Inventor of Frozen-Food Process." New York Times, October 9, 1956.

Cobb, Emma. "Notes from the Field." Invention & Technology, Fall 1987.

Coe, Brian. "William Friese Greene and the Origins of Kinematography: Part I." Photographic Journal, March 1962.

Coffman, Cathy. "Tough Teflon® Trivia." Automotive Industries, June 1988.

"Conrad Hubert, 70, Died in France." New York Times, March 18, 1928.

Crouch, Tom D. "How the Bicycle Took Wing." Invention & Technology, Summer 1986.

Culhane, John, and T. H. Culhane. "The Master Modeler: Leonardo as a Lifelong Inspiration." Science Digest, December 1985.

David, Lester. "Why Didn't I Think of That?" American Legion, March 1990.

de Kruif, Paul. "Boss Kettering." Saturday Evening Post, July 15, 1933.

Fadiman, Anne. "Joe Newman: The Enigmatic Energy Man." Life, September 1986.

Fincher, Jack. "George Ferris' Wheel of Fortune." Smithsonian, July 1983.

Forbes, Malcolm. "They Went That-a-Way." Saturday Evening Post, May-June 1989.

Freedman, David H. "Cosmic Time Travel." Discover, June 1989.

Friedel, Robert. "New Light on Edison's Light." Invention & Technology, Summer 1985.

Gatty, Bob. "Mishaps That Mothered Invention." Nation's Business, Vol. 75, no. 2.

Gies, Joseph. "The Great Reaper War." Invention & Technology, Winter 1990.

Golden, Frederic. "Big Dimwits and Little Geniuses." Time, January 3, 1983.

Gould, Stephen Jay. "This View of Life." Natural History, July 1989.

Gutman, Dan. "Pixel Pioneers." Science Digest, December 1983.

Hall, Stephen S. "A Lightning Rod for Praise and Blame." Smithsonian, June 1986.

Harrington, Mark W. "Weather Making, Ancient and Modern." National Geographic, April 25, 1894.

Huffman, Dale. "Ermal Fraze, Inventor of Pop Top, Dies." Dayton Daily News, October 27, 1989.

Hug, René. "George de Mestral." London Independent, February 19, 1990.

Hughes, Thomas P. "How Did the Heroic Inventors Do It?" Invention & Technology, Fall 1985.

Jackson, Donald Dale. "While He Expected the Worst, Nobel Hoped for the Best." Smithsonian, November 1988.

Josephy, Alvin M., Jr., "Those Pants That Levi Gave Us." American West, July-August 1985.

Kahn, David. "Cryptology and the Origins of Spread Spectrum." IEEE Spectrum, September 1964.

Ketteringham, John M., and P. Ranganath Nayak. "People Behind the Wonders." Reader's Digest, July 1987.

Langford, John S. "Triumph of Daedalus." National Geographic, August 1988.

Long, Michael E. "The Flight of the Gossamer Condor." National Geographic, January 1978.

Mikelbank, Peter. "Changing the Corset of History." Washington Post, March 29, 1989.

Narvaez, Alfonso A. "E. C. Fraze, 76; Devised Pull Tab." New York Times, October 28, 1989.

"Newman's Impossible Motor." Science, February 10, 1984.

"Ooh-la-la! The Bra." Life, June 1989.

Petroski, Henry. "H. D. Thoreau, Engineer." Invention & Technology, Fall 1989.

Plunkett, Roy J. "Happy Birthday, Teflon." Design News, April 18, 1988.

Reese, K. M. "How Teenage Chemist Found Path to Fortune." Chemical & Engineering News,

February 13, 1989.

Shaw, David. "What Bill Lear Wants, Bill Lear Invents." *Esquire,* September 1972.

Snow, Richard F. "They're Still There." *Invention & Technology,* Summer 1986.

Stone, Judith. "On the Rodent Again." *Discover,* November 1989.

Tierney, John. "Perpetual Commotion." *Science,* May 1983.

Travis, A. S. "Mauve and Alizarin: William Perkin's Contributions to the Modern Chemical Industry." *Steam,* July 1988.

Updike, John. "A Critic at Large (Benjamin Franklin)." *New Yorker,* February 22, 1988.

Weiner, Mark. "Rocketing Rollerblades: In-Line Skates Are the Latest Rage." *Washington Post,* May 5, 1989.

Other Sources

"General Information Concerning Patents." Washington, D.C.: U.S. Department of Commerce, April 1989.

Narin, Francis, and Dominic Olivastro. "Identifying Areas of Leading Edge Japanese Science and Technology." NSF Grant No. SRS-8507306. Haddon Heights, N.J.: CHI Research/Computer Horizons, Inc., April 15, 1988.

"The Story of the U.S. Patent and Trademark Office." Washington, D.C.: U.S. Department of Commerce, August 1988.

"The Story of Xerography." Stamford, Conn.: Xerox Corporation, no date.

"Technology Assessment & Forecast." Program Brochure. Washington, D.C.: U.S. Department of Commerce, May 6, 1988.

INDEX

Numerals in italics indicate an illustration of the subject mentioned.

Time-Life Books Inc.
is a wholly owned subsidiary of
THE TIME INC. BOOK COMPANY

TIME-LIFE BOOKS INC.

Managing Editor: Thomas H. Flaherty
Director of Editorial Resources:
Elise D. Ritter-Clough
Director of Photography and Research:
John Conrad Weiser
Editorial Board: Dale Brown, Roberta Conlan,
Laura Foreman, Lee Hassig, Jim Hicks,
Blaine Marshall, Rita Mullin, Henry Woodhead

PUBLISHER: Joseph J. Ward

Editorial Director: Russell B. Adams, Jr.
Marketing Director: Anne C. Everhart
Director of Design: Louis Klein
Production Manager: Prudence G. Harris
Supervisor of Quality Control: James King

Editorial Operations
Production: Celia Beattie
Library: Louise D. Forstall
Computer Composition: Deborah G. Tait (Manager),
Monika D. Thayer, Janet Barnes Syring,
Lillian Daniels

**Library of Congress
Cataloging-in-Publication Data**
Inventive Genius / by the editors of Time-Life Books.
p.   cm.   (Library of curious and unusual facts)
Includes bibliographical references.
ISBN 0-8094-7699-1 (trade)
ISBN 0-8094-7700-9 (lib. bdg.)
1. Inventors—Biography.
I. Time-Life Books. II. Series.
T39.I57 1991
609.2′2—dc20   90-11264 CIP

LIBRARY OF CURIOUS AND UNUSUAL FACTS

SERIES EDITORS: Russell B. Adams, Jr.,
Laura Foreman
Series Administrator: Elise D. Ritter-Clough
Art Director: Susan K. White
Picture Editor: Sally Collins

Editorial Staff for *Inventive Genius*
Text Editor: Carl A. Posey
Associate Editor/Research: Robert H. Wooldridge, Jr.
(principal), Catherine M. Chase, Roxie France-
Nuriddin, Maureen McHugh
Associate Editor/Researcher/Writer: Susan Arritt
Assistant Art Director: Alan Pitts
Copy Coordinators: Jarelle S. Stein (principal),
Donna Carey
Picture Coordinator: Jennifer Iker
Editorial Assistant: Terry Ann Paredes

Special Contributors: Joe Alper, Leslie Marshall,
George Russell, Chuck Smith (text); Norma Shaw,
Vicki Warren, Beth Winters (research); Linda Falk
(index).

Correspondents: Elisabeth Kraemer-Singh (Bonn),
Christine Hinze (London), Christina Lieberman (New
York), Maria Vincenza Aloisi (Paris), Ann Natanson
(Rome).
Valuable assistance was also provided by Brigid
Grauman (Brussels), Judy Aspinall (London), Wibo
Van de Linde (Netherlands), Elizabeth Brown (New
York), Dag Christensen (Oslo), Josephine du Brusle
(Paris), Ann Wise (Rome), Dick Berry, Mieko Ikeda
(Tokyo).

The Consultants:
William R. Corliss, the general consultant for the
series, is a physicist-turned-writer who has spent the
last twenty-five years compiling collections of
anomalies in the fields of geophysics, geology, ar-
chaeology, astronomy, biology, and psychology. He
has written about science and technology for NASA,
the National Science Foundation, and the Energy
Research and Development Administration (among
others). Mr. Corliss is also the author of more than
thirty books on scientific mysteries, including *Mysterious Universe, The Unfathomed Mind,* and *Hand-
book of Unusual Natural Phenomena.*

Robert Friedel, associate professor of history at the
University of Maryland in College Park, Maryland,
teaches courses on the history of technology and
the history of science. He has been a historian at
the Smithsonian Institution and director of the Center for the History of Electrical Engineering. Among
his books are *Edison's Electric Light: Biography of
an Invention* and *Pioneer Plastic: The Making and
Selling of Celluloid.*

Marcello Truzzi, a professor of sociology at Eastern
Michigan University, is director of the Center for
Scientific Anomalies Research (CSAR) and editor of
its journal, *Zetetic Scholar.*

Other Publications:

AMERICAN COUNTRY
VOYAGE THROUGH THE UNIVERSE
THE THIRD REICH
THE TIME-LIFE GARDENER'S GUIDE
MYSTERIES OF THE UNKNOWN
TIME FRAME
FIX IT YOURSELF
FITNESS, HEALTH & NUTRITION
SUCCESSFUL PARENTING
HEALTHY HOME COOKING
UNDERSTANDING COMPUTERS
LIBRARY OF NATIONS
THE ENCHANTED WORLD
THE KODAK LIBRARY OF CREATIVE PHOTOGRAPHY
GREAT MEALS IN MINUTES
THE CIVIL WAR
PLANET EARTH
COLLECTOR'S LIBRARY OF THE CIVIL WAR
THE EPIC OF FLIGHT
THE GOOD COOK
WORLD WAR II
HOME REPAIR AND IMPROVEMENT
THE OLD WEST

For information on and a full description of any of
the Time-Life Books series listed above, please call
1-800-621-7026 or write:
Reader Information
Time-Life Customer Service
P.O. Box C-32068
Richmond, Virginia 23261-2068

This volume is one in a series that explores
astounding but surprisingly true events in history,
science, nature, and human conduct. Other books in
the series include:

Feats and Wisdom of the Ancients
Mysteries of the Human Body
Forces of Nature
Vanishings
Amazing Animals

Time-Life Books Inc. offers a wide range of fine re-
cordings, including a *Rock 'n' Roll Era* series. For
subscription information, call 1-800-621-7026 or
write Time-Life Music, P.O. Box C-32068, Richmond,
Virginia 23261-2068.

TIME
LIFE
BOOKS